PRAISE FOR
SPARKED

"Move over, MBTI! There's a new personality index in town. The Sparketypes will illuminate what work lights you up!"

—NEIL PASRICHA,
New York Times bestselling author of
The Book of Awesome and *The Happiness Equation*

"If you've ever wondered why you run into the same obstacles at work, no matter your role or responsibilities, Jonathan Fields's new book offers you a precise roadmap for understanding this important truth: It's not you. It's your expectation that you should be able to do things the way others do. When you understand your unique *Sparked* blueprint, you encounter a world of possibility you had not imagined. Based on his years of experience as an entrepreneur and countless conversations about The Good Life with experts in many disciplines, he shows you the way to meaningful work, creative confidence, and the knowledge you are doing exactly what you're meant to."

—SUSAN PIVER,
New York Times bestselling author
of *The Four Noble Truths of Love*

"The framework contained within this book has the revelatory power of one-on-one therapy or coaching. But instead of waiting years for a breakthrough, it comes in minutes. The more I learned about my Sparketype (and just as importantly, my Anti-Sparketype), the more I was able to put into words things I've always known deep down to be true but couldn't readily give shape to. As a business leader being constantly pulled in a million directions, I finally feel I have clarity on where I should put my energy and the permission to focus on where I'll have the most impact. I'll be getting copies for my whole team!"

—EMILY HEYWARD,
Cofounder of Red Antler

"I've worked with a lot of models before, but no framework has gotten my community more aligned and on fire as quickly as the Sparketype model. It transcends jobs and roles to help people figure out the right game to be playing for them. Get the book, learn your Sparketype, and start finishing your best work today."

—CHARLIE GILKEY,
Author of the award-winning *Start Finishing*

"With more than twenty-five years developing employees and creating great employee experiences, one thing has become clear to me: People want more than just a paycheck. They want to be excited, be inspired, and have a sense of purpose. *Sparked* is the ultimate guide for leaders, founders, and those who want more out of work and life."

—DEB JOSEPHS,
Chief People Officer at Latch

"This book has the capacity to shift the way we show up in the world. Jonathan Fields has created a groundbreaking tool that is profoundly important and necessary for each one of us. We often move through the world on autopilot hoping to one day find ourselves and better understand the work we're meant to do. In the meantime, life simply passes us by. Until now. *Sparked* offers the tools for and insight into fulfilling your potential and purpose based on who you inherently are. It guides you to recognize what energizes and inspires you but also offers insights into where you struggle most deeply. It is the compass that we all need, served up in a format that is both easily digestible and deeply insightful. It will bring about realizations, a deeper understanding of self, and much-needed inspiration too."

—CYNDIE SPIEGEL,
Author of *A Year of Positive Thinking*
and Founder of Dear Grown Ass Women®

SPARKED

Discover Your Unique Imprint for Work That Makes You Come Alive

JONATHAN FIELDS

HarperCollins
Leadership

An Imprint of HarperCollins

Published by HarperCollins Leadership, an imprint of HarperCollins Focus LLC.

Any internet addresses, phone numbers, or company or product information printed in this book are offered as a resource and are not intended in any way to be or to imply an endorsement by HarperCollins Leadership, nor does HarperCollins Leadership vouch for the existence, content, or services of these sites, phone numbers, companies, or products beyond the life of this book.

The author and publisher have worked to ensure that the information in his book was correct at press time, however, the author and publisher do not assume and hereby disclaim any liability to any party for any loss, damage, or disruption caused by errors or omissions, whether such errors or omissions result from negligence, accident, or any other case. This book offers personal development guidance and information and is designed for educational purposes only. You should not rely on this information as a substitute for, nor does it replace, the advice of a professional or your personal advisors. The use of any information provided in this book is solely at your own risk. If you wish to apply ideas contained in this guidebook, the author and publisher assume no responsibility for your actions. The information in this book is not meant as a substitute for direct assistance by a qualified expert. If direct assistance is advised, the services of a qualified professional should be sought.

ISBN 978-1-4002-2549-1 (eBook)
ISBN 978-1-4002-2546-0 (HC)

Library of Congress Control Number: 2021941069

Printed in the United States of America
21 22 23 24 25 LSC 10 9 8 7 6 5 4 3 2 1

To all who feel the call to come alive.
It's our time.

CONTENTS

A NOTE FROM JONATHAN

Hey there.

Before you dive into this book, a quick heads-up . . .

You're about to discover some things about yourself, your work, and your life that'll open your eyes to an entirely new universe of possibilities.

And you may also, maybe for the first time ever, find yourself deeply seen, understood, and equipped to step into the world of work in a profoundly different, deeply rewarding way.

That is amazing. It's the whole point of the work I've been doing for years, and, well, a big part of why this book exists.

But, I have to bring your attention to something, and ask a quick favor.

When you start to see what's possible in the realm of work, how it can fill you with meaning, energy, excitement, purpose, and that deeply nourishing sense of realized potential, you may also have this urge to blow everything up and start fresh.

Please, do not do this!

That approach may be appropriate for some folks, but it's often the absolute wrong call for many, even most, others. And you'll likely not know which you are until you've read the book and learned when, why, and how to explore the different paths to Sparking your work and life based on your unique Sparke-type and circumstance. Truth is, most people will discover something they never expected. You can come more fully alive right where you are, by just approaching your work and life with deeper wisdom and a new set of tools.

So, please, hold off on doing anything big and disruptive. Much will be revealed as you deepen into the insights and discover how best to Spark your work and, in turn, your life!

Okay, now, read on. So much to discover. So much life to live into!

With a whole lotta
love and gratitude,

Jonathan

ACKNOWLEDGMENTS

This book is built upon a set of ideas that have been percolating for decades. Still, going from concept to creation takes a village, made up of different people and, yes, different Sparketypes. To Sara Kendrick (Essentialist/Maven) and the team at Harper-Collins Leadership, thanks for believing in this work, not laughing when I handed you a 125,000-word manuscript, and, instead, helping me turn it into something human, valuable, and beautiful. To Scott Hoffman (Scientist/Maven) and Jan Baumer (Nurturer/Advisor) at Folio Literary Management, what an experience we had, sharing this book with the publishing world at a time nobody knew what the next day might hold. Grateful for your vision, effort, and trust in me and the idea.

To Lindsey Fox (Essentialist/Nurturer), podcast producer extraordinaire and overseer of all things complex and creative, your ability to keep all the plates spinning and, somehow, to allow me to feel held along the way has been a true gift. To Shelley Adelle (Performer/Maker), so appreciate your devotion and embrace of almost anything in the name of making good things happen. To Courtney Kenney (Maker/Maven), I cannot imagine what the process of bringing this book to the world would've looked like without you. To Sutton Long (Scientist/

Maker), thankful for your always thoughtful and generous design lens and big, kind heart. To Scott Meola (Maker/Maven), appreciate your efforts to help make this book not just valuable but beautiful.

To my chosen family, all the texts, calls, DMs, emojis, emails, walks, hugs, ideas, and dark chocolate interventions during one of the strangest times in history to be writing a book about work, life, meaning, and possibility has been everything. To the wonderful folks who shared stories and insights featured in this book, and to those who were equally generous yet not able to be included, huge thanks. To the giant community of individuals and organizations who've supported this work, thanks for continuing to make it all possible.

To Stephanie (Maker/Advocate), this has been a season we'll never forget. I cannot begin to share how blessed I feel to be telling this story side by side. Love you tons. And, to Jesse, so much of what's in these pages has been inspired by the world and sense of possibility I hope to help you inherit. My heart is in your hands, always was, always will be. This one's for you.

WHAT SHOULD I DO
WITH MY LIFE?

Type "what should I do" into Google, and there's a decent chance it'll finish your sentence "with my life."

If you're feeling a bit lost or have no clear sense of what you're here to do, you're not alone. Millions are right there with you, searching for an answer to the same question, yet never quite finding it.

This perpetual discontent shows up in our personal and professional lives as anxiety, futility, disengagement, malaise, and manifests in many other physical and emotional ways. It affects not just how we feel, but also how we show up in our work, our relationships, and our lives. Our focus is scattered, we know we're not performing anywhere near our potential, and there's this nagging lack of purpose and possibility that feels like a perpetual drag in our systems. Maybe you've felt some or all of that.

We hate feeling this way, knowing we are capable of so much more—"meant" for so much more—yet having no idea what that looks like, let alone how to live it. We keep searching for a way out, a different job, industry, or lifestyle. But that's not the answer. While circumstance is part of the equation, the bigger switch that often needs to be flipped is one of self-discovery. We can't know where to steer our lives until we better understand what makes us come alive, and what empties us out.

It all starts with one central question, *"What am I here to do?"*

When most of us ask, we're thinking about work. What is my unique contribution? To my life. To the lives of those around me. To society. Whether it's the thing I get paid to do, or the thing, once discovered, I can't *not* do, simply because it's the air that breathes me.

What is the essential nature of the work I'm here to do?

This book is your first giant step into a level of understanding, validation, and, for many, revelation that holds the key to a different way to approach your work, living, and life. An approach that bridges the gap from just getting by to coming alive.

For more than two decades, I've immersed myself in the study of human potential, collaborating with and studying everyone from academic researchers to leading voices in a wide array of fields — from social sciences to functional medicine, human performance, excellence, and expertise, positive-psychology, and more. Along the way, I've founded and built a series of wellness companies; developed frameworks and protocols; launched and grown the Good Life Project global community, organization, and top-ranked podcast; taught thousands of students; and worked with emerging and senior leaders and amazing humans from all walks of life. All the while, I've been on a quest to discover what allows people to find or create work that makes them come alive and maximizes their potential.

Working with my team over the last five years, we began to focus more intensely on this state that I call "being Sparked," especially in the context of work. I've come to realize that being Sparked exists at the sweet spot between five domains:

- **Purpose.** Knowing you're moving toward something you believe in.
- **Engagement.** Excitement, energy, and enthusiasm for the pursuit of that something.
- **Meaningfulness.** The feeling that what you do and who you are matters.
- **Expressed potential.** The sensation of being fully you and not having to hide, bringing all of your potential to the experience, and leaving nothing untapped.
- **Flow.** The blissful experience of getting lost in an activity, losing time, and becoming absorbed in the task.

Early in life, it turns out, we begin to exhibit a certain unique *imprint* or *affinity*—an intrinsic impulse—for work that makes us come alive. This work gives us the feeling of being Sparked. These imprints not only determine what type of work or effort we're drawn to (and repelled from), they also tend to come with a host of common behaviors, quirks, and attachments. I call these imprints "Sparketypes®," which is an easy shorthand for the source code level driver of work that makes you come alive. Not just for now, but for life.

For most people, discovering your Sparketype is like meeting your true self. There is an immediate, intuitive knowing—an undeniable truth that explains so many past choices and out-comes. It empowers you to not only understand who you are and why you do what you do, but also how you contribute to the world on a very different, more intentional, and fulfilling level.

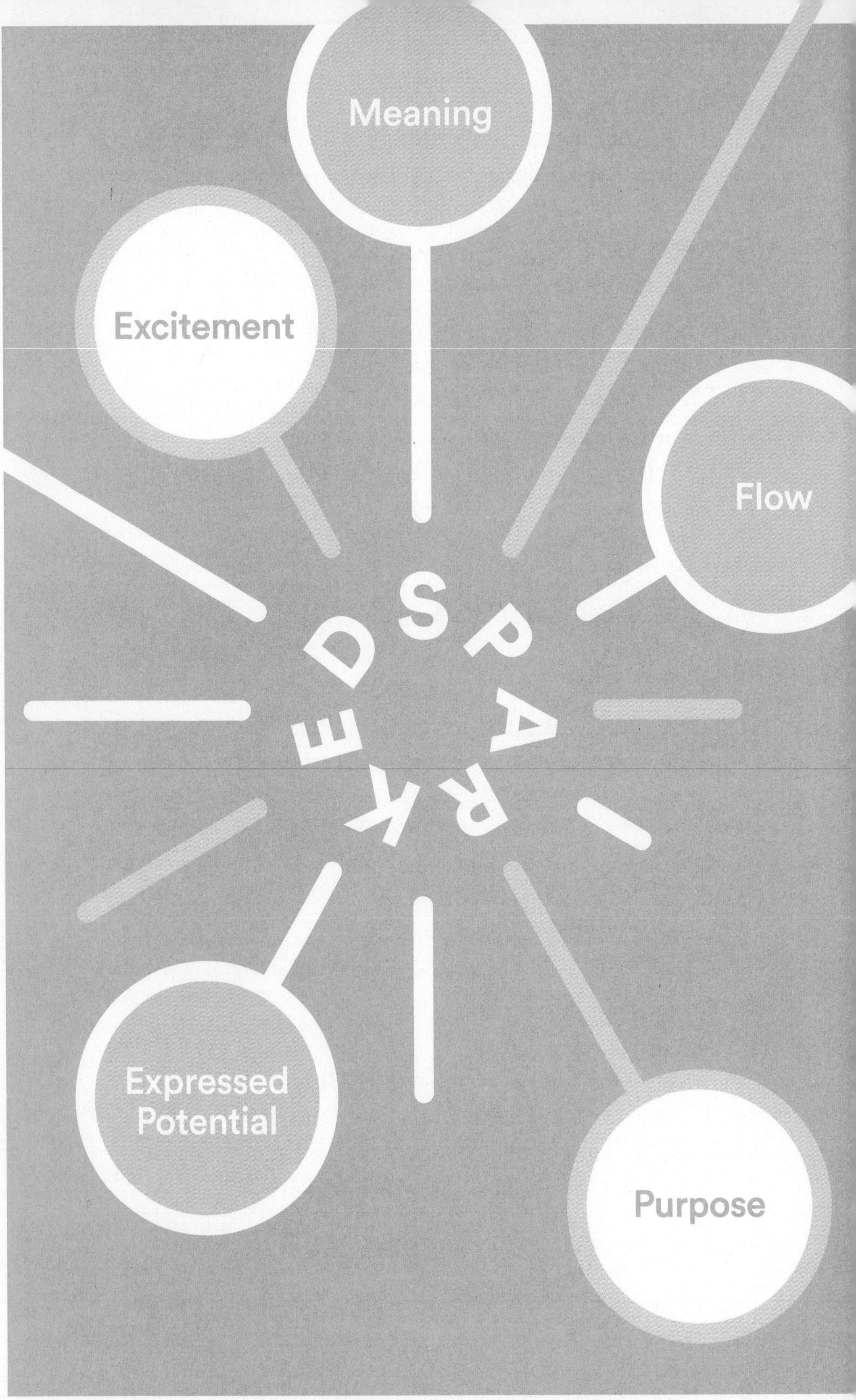
Meaning
Excitement
Flow
SPARKED
Expressed Potential
Purpose

It sparks your life and ignites those around you. Discovering your Sparketype is often described as a "homecoming." A recognition that, "yes, this *is* me, and it's worthy of my time, energy, and attention."

While words like "life purpose" or "singular passion" often lead people down a path of confusion and futility, rather than clarity and action, finding your Sparketype gives you the exact opposite. It equips you with insight that immediately rings true, a sense of direction, and the freedom to finally lead from a place of truth and potential. It allows you to let go of a lifetime of scattered and perpetually unfulfilling wheel-spinning. It frees you from all the less-nourishing distractions, and allows you to devote your energy to finding the incredible, vast kaleidoscope of pursuits, careers, projects, and adventures that let you express your unique imprint on a level that makes you come more fully alive.

You don't have to buy into any one origin story, catchphrase, or set of beliefs to experience the self-evident, sustained nature and guiding influence of your Sparketype. You just have to discover yours, then weave it into the way you live and give. The feeling it gives back to you, the way those around you begin to respond when you live, play, and work from this place, will be all the validation, all the proof you need.

Now, of course, a few questions immediately arise.

HOW MANY SPARKETYPES ARE THERE?

The quick answer is ten. Funny enough, we began with a slightly larger number, 7.8 billion, the number of people in the world. We're each unique, so there must also be 7.8 billion unique imprints. We cannot be distilled, right? Not so fast.

Your Sparketype is a bit like your DNA. On the surface, it may express itself in billions of unique, gloriously-you-and-only-you ways. But when you start to peel each person's purpose, engagement, meaning, expression, and flow onion, billions of valid, surface-level, time-limited, circumstance-driven expressions reduce down to a remarkably small set of source code level elements or imprints. This leaves us with ten distinct DNA-level drivers. The Sparketypes.

| MAVEN | MAKER | SCIENTIST | ESSENTIALIST | PERFORMER |

| SAGE | WARRIOR | ADVISOR | ADVOCATE | NURTURER |

YOUR SPARKETYPE HAS THREE ELEMENTS.

We're all a blend of a number of different Sparketypes, but every person has a distinct Sparketype Profile that is made up of three key components. These represent your strongest impulses at both ends of the spectrum, the work that fills you up, as well as empties you out.

- Your Primary Sparketype. Think of your Primary Sparketype as the thing that generates the strongest impulse to exert effort for no other reason than the fact that it makes you feel alive. It is the underlying driver or source-fuel for the work that gives you the readiest access to flow, energizes and excites you, gives you a sense of meaning and purpose, and allows you to feel like you're expressing your fullest self and potential. Expressed in a healthy and constructive way, it's a big part of any number of jobs, experiences, hobbies, passions, and devotions that make you come alive, even when the work is hard.

- Your Shadow Sparketype. Your Shadow Sparketype is also a big part of you, sometimes even a close second behind your Primary. It is not, however, your strongest impulse. It's easy to think of your Shadow Sparketype as your "runner-up" Sparketype. And, it may be a very close second. But, while there is a lot of truth to that, a much more nuanced and important-to-understand relationship almost always exists between your Primary and your Shadow. Your Shadow Sparketype most often reveals the work that you may well enjoy and have developed a high level of skill around—but, when you're really being honest, it is also the work you do largely in service of doing the work of your Primary Sparketype better. Think of it as your Primary Sparketype amplifier.

- Your Anti-Sparketype. Your Anti-Sparketype is the type of work that is the heaviest lift for you. It takes the most out of you, and requires the greatest amount of recovery even if, objectively, it's not that hard. There's just something about it that leaves you empty, as opposed to making you come alive.

Your Primary and Shadow are your inner collaborators.

I am a Maker Primary with a Scientist Shadow. This is a common pairing. (As is the reverse.) My main impulse, the thing that fills me up even when it's really hard, is making things. At any given time, outward expressions of this could find me building a guitar, writing a book, or even launching a company.

With every quest to create, at many points along the way, I find myself drawing upon my Scientist Shadow Sparketype to help me make whatever I'm working on better. There are always hard questions to be answered, puzzles to be solved, tools, systems, and more to be designed. The act of creation is often constrained by limitations in tools, processes, tech, resources, and so much more. Figuring these things out along the way is largely the work of the Scientist, who is driven by the pursuit of answers to burning questions, solving problems, and figuring out puzzles.

Over the years, I've become very good at the work of my Scientist Shadow. It's not so much that I've wanted to, it's that I had to in order to be a better Maker. I tap my problem-solving impulse in the quest to make better tools, processes, and experiences that help people come alive. This is especially true for solitary pursuits or in the early days of bootstrapped startups where I've had to play all roles because I didn't have the money to bring in a team yet. At the end of the day, while it's satisfying to solve problems and find answers, that process is not my reason for being. For me, it's largely in service of my fierce yearning to create, to make ideas manifest. It's not about the answer to the question, it's about what that answer allows me to make.

How can I validate this? Pretty simple, actually. The moment I've figured out enough of a solution to let me make better things, I turn back to the process of making. I'm done being a Scientist and entirely back into the all-consuming generative space of creation.

Your Anti-Sparketype is your work "lead weight."

Discovering your Primary and Shadow Sparketypes and how they work together is key, but understanding your Anti-Sparketype is equally important. When you know your full profile, all three elements, it helps you decide not only what to run toward, but also what to run from. Even if it's work you have to do for your job, at least you'll better understand why it takes so much effort and leaves you so empty, and can better prepare yourself for the task, allocate space for recovery, and find ways to delegate or minimize it whenever and wherever possible.

HOW DO YOU DISCOVER YOUR SPARKETYPE?

This is where things get even more interesting. Some people stumble upon their Sparketype on their own. This tends to happen in one of two ways.

- Through fortune, they just happen to be exposed to something that sparks them early in life, then have the rare depth of self-awareness, guidance, and commitment to self-inquiry that allows them to understand what was revealed to them.

- They embrace a process of deliberate experimentation, trying on different types of work, taking notes, then zeroing in on the types of things that give them that feeling of coming alive. This approach often unfolds over a period of decades.

These individuals and experiences are incredibly rare. Many people understand that a certain type of activity or job makes them feel a certain way, but they don't know why, and can't easily reproduce that feeling in pursuits, jobs, organizations, or industries. This may be you, and if it is, you're in the right place.

Even more often, people have no real sense at all for the type of work that makes them come alive. No clear understanding of what that deeper impulse is that might allow them to feel—to know—they're doing the work they're here to do. No sense of how to discover that DNA-level driver of effort that lights them up, and keeps them sparked for life.

WELCOME TO THE SPARKETYPE ASSESSMENT®.

Realizing this huge gap in awareness, we set out to develop a tool—the Sparketype Assessment—that would allow anyone, anywhere, to rapidly discover their Sparketype. While it took more than a year to develop (and that grew out of decades of prior investigation, collaboration, and integration), this online assessment can be completed in a matter of minutes. It takes the average person about ten or twelve minutes and it reveals your full Sparketype profile—all three elements. If you haven't already discovered it, you can find it now at Sparketype.com.

The moment of truth.

Since launching the platform, more than 500,000 individuals and organizations have tapped the power of the Sparketype Assessment. The wisdom accumulated and massive data-set (more than 25 million data-points) has revealed powerful insights not just for individuals, but also for organizations, leaders, and beyond. Beyond the data, the deluge of stories, insights, and feedback from people all over the world has been stunning:

> I've been working in career development and coaching for almost twenty years. I'm using it with everyone that I coach and train and they love it too! Big, big gratitude for all your work!"

> I run the first-year experience courses at a university and I taught two classes in the fall. I had all of my students do the Sparketype test. They loved it and it even inspired one student to change her major! This work is powerful. My students loved having a new take on who they are through the Sparketypes."

> I do a lot of research on self-development and growth, and nothing has touched me quite like everything you guys are doing. The Sparketype Assessment and your insight has helped free my mind. I am and always will be grateful."

"Wow! I took your profile and answered the questions. I am BLOWN AWAY!!!! Thank you for communicating words to me that I totally relate to, because it's who I am as a HUMAN!!! You have affected my life in an incredibly profound and deep way today."

"I took the Sparketype test. I learned that I'm an Advisor. I wasn't surprised by this result, yet, it was something I hadn't ever thought about before! This is something I could lean into, whatever I do. With this knowledge at hand, I recently started my own blog (on the side of my nine-to-five job) to share my own wisdom and stories with others. I've never felt happier and more alive, truly. I've been jumping out of bed early each morning to work on the blog before I head to work!"

"I'm a stay-at-home mom who was homeschooling my three children full time until last year. Now my two oldest have transitioned to a part-time homeschool/school and my youngest (four) is still at home with me. I've been trying to figure out what I want to do next and my Sparketype results have been a wonderful resource for that."

"Even though I have done a LOT of personality typing work (I mean a LOT), for some reason your framework has been more illuminating than any other. The idea that my shadow Sparketype is in service of my primary was like YES, that's it!"

"The Sparketype info has already changed how I feel about myself, and what I had always thought of as a failing (Maven/Maker) and had been told by many people was, basically, a procrastination exercise—to read that my zest for knowledge IS who I am, was utterly redemptive! Thank you!"

Woot! Woot! Holy awesomeness! CANNOT wait to find out more and to be able to put everything I'm learning into practice. Sparketypes have been so much more insightful than any other type of "personality" test I've ever taken including Myers-Briggs. Thank you so much for all the hard work Jonathan and team!!"

The response has been incredible, but so, too, has the demand for a bigger toolbox that reveals many more layers of understanding and points you, more clearly, toward action.

THIS BOOK TAKES YOU DEEPER AND SHOWS YOU HOW TO RISE HIGHER.

The Sparketype Assessment delivers the "source code level" answer to the question that tens of millions of people ask every day: "What should I do with my life?" *SPARKED* builds on this DNA, giving you a more robust, comprehensive understanding of your unique imprint, how to leverage it, what it looks like when leveraged in a healthy way, where you're most likely to be triggered and stumble, and how you relate to others and build action around it.

HOW DO YOU READ AND USE THIS BOOK?

For many people, *SPARKED* is not a book you'll read from end to end. Think of it more as the ultimate reference manual and action plan for creating the rest of your life.

The following ten chapters are all about you. Well, and those you love, play with, create with, work with, lead, and pretty much anyone else you want to get to know better. All ten chapters share the same structure, taking you much deeper into each Sparketype. You'll also learn how each one is nourished and stifled, what you need to feel fulfilled, where you tend to get tripped up and why, what it looks like when you're heading toward a major stumble and what to do about it. You'll learn how certain Sparketype pairings tend to show up, how each tends to find an outlet, and how that outlet can lead to a career and generate an income. And you'll meet others who share your Sparketype and see how they've worked with that Sparketype in real-life and work situations, so you can learn from and become inspired by them.

Safe bet, given human nature, you'll flip first to the chapter about your Primary Sparketype, then your Shadow, then your Anti-Sparketype. That's great. Dive in. Learn about the essential impulses and how they fuel your feelings and actions (often in ways you never noticed or understood). If you're curious, be sure to have your partner, spouse, friends, family, colleagues, and collaborators complete the Sparketype Assessment. Then you can all explore your profiles and share how you've seen the different elements show up in each other. Revel in those chapters, learn from them, then build meaningful conversation around them. Use them as a tool not just to come alive, but to deepen your connection and understanding of those around you—and their understanding of you.

Do not, however, skip the chapter that follows the ten Sparketype-specific ones. It contains pretty important and I'd even say contrarian insights about how to bring your Sparketype to the world, how not to, and how to navigate the real-world tension that sometimes arises between adult responsibilities and your desire to come more fully alive.

Finally, I'll leave you with an invitation. Do not just *read* this book. *Use* it. Let it be your first step in a process of discovery, awakening, liberation, connection, and impact. Allow it to fuel your own inner rising, your own coming alive. Then, share it all and bring those you care about, work alongside, and collaborate with along with you.

Onward, then—let's get Sparked!

YOU'RE ABOUT TO ENTER
THE REALM OF THE
SPARKETYPES!

Before you proceed, please be sure you've completed your Sparketype Assessment to ensure what you discover is as personal and relevant as possible.

You can find the assessment at
SPARKETYPE.COM

Or you can just hold most mobile-device cameras over the QR code below and they will instantly pull up the webpage for you.

THE
MAVEN

You, in a Nutshell.

SLOGAN.
I live to learn.

Animating impulse.

Mavens are all about learning. Often on a level that goes beyond curiosity and lands as fascination, even obsession. Can't. Stop. Learning.

As a Maven, you're fueled by a near-primal drive to know more, even if there is no end beyond simply scratching your often misunderstood and sometimes maligned "that is insanely cool, I must know more" itch. The thing that gets you out of bed in the morning is the opportunity to go to sleep knowing more than you did the day before. You view learning as an almost sacred pursuit, one you easily get lost in.

In fact, because the opportunities to learn are often so abundant, internal, and unimpeded, Mavens drop more readily into that blissed-out, time-fugued state of flow than other Sparketypes. They sink into an eight-hundred-page biography, follow a

Google search about the mating patterns of dinosaurs, or tear through a bingeworthy lineup of documentaries on a Sunday morning only to look up and wonder if it's time for breakfast . . . at 11:00 p.m.

Mavens tend to be extremely process-driven. For them, it's not about reaching a place where they know all there is to know about a subject. In fact, the end of the learning road is often a melancholy experience, which is why you'll often find the most-fulfilled Mavens are the ones fueled more by either a broad fascination with everyone and everything, or a more focused impulse to learn about a field that is so deep or complex, the learning well will never run dry. Either way, the opportunity to do the thing they're here to do never ends. When working in a way that allows them the resources and control to spend the greatest amount of time immersed in the process of learning, deepening into a broad or narrow fascination, focused on a topic they feel innately drawn to, Mavens feel most alive. They become *fully expressed*. Sparked.

Broad Fascination.

The Maven impulse sometimes shows up as a generalized, relentless curiosity about everything and everyone, like you live in a state of childlike wonder about the world around you. My friend Neil Pasricha (Maven/Maker) personifies this. A Maven Primary, he's one of the most genuinely and broadly curious people I know. If he asks how you're doing, he waits for an answer. Then, he asks why. What contributed to it? How do you feel about your answer? he'll wonder. And, would it have been different yesterday?

Does he want to know because he cares about me? Sure. I mean, we're friends. But there's something else going on. He is deeply fascinated with people, often total strangers, and what makes them tick on every level. Why we do the things we do. He yearns to know the entirety of the human experience. And he will talk to anyone and everyone about it. For Neil, every interaction is a moment of micro-discovery. Another drop in his bottomless Maven tank.

Narrow and deep.

While the Maven's impulse to learn often shows up as a broad-based fascination, other times this knowledge quest finds an outlet in the pursuit of specific topics or fields of interest. It's all about the ability to go narrow and deep—to drink from a well, and the best wells are the ones that never run dry.

Another friend, Dimple Mukherjee (Maven/Nurturer), has earned her living as an occupational therapist her entire adult life. Over the last few years, she's added a growing coaching practice, primarily focusing on women in their middle years, creating more of a blended career path. Fueling her outward devotion to service, which is how she earns her living (a manifestation of her Nurturer Shadow), is a fierce drive to learn. She devours everything she can that touches, in some way, on helping people move from suffering, whether related to physical or psychological pain, into a place of grace and ease. Degrees, licenses, trainings, certifications, immersions, she's done them all, and will continue to seek knowledge in this specific domain, likely for life.

Does this deepening reservoir of wisdom make her better in her chosen career? Absolutely. But it also serves another, less apparent, purpose. It quenches her Maven's lifelong desire to learn. To know. To keep going deeper and getting wiser. For

Dimple, because she's found her way into a complex, ever-branching, and vast body of knowledge—understanding and helping people move from suffering to flourishing—the opportunity to exist in a state of perpetual discovery can never be truly exhausted. She'll never reach the end of her curiosity.

The Blend.

Then, of course, there's the middle or blended Maven's path. This can show up as some mix of narrow and deep, shallow and wide—or even a series of semi-deep dives. This last manifestation, where you seem to "float" from fascination to fascination, learning what you need, then moving on, can sometimes be tricky. In large part because of the way others may perceive—and judge—you. On the inside, you're getting everything you need. You find something fascinating, dive in, immerse yourself in learning everything there is to know, then move on. In your mind, you did what you came to do. In the minds of those who see but don't get you, it's often a different story.

Techla Wood (Maven/Maker) is a fun example. A stay-at-home mom who'd been home-educating her kids for more than two decades, she found her way into a series of mini knowledge quests over the years. One day, she discovered chocolate. Okay, so maybe she already knew about chocolate. I am 100 percent convinced we're all born with a prior knowledge of chocolate and spend our entire lives in search of the perfect bar. In Techla's case, she stumbled into the world of raw chocolate-making. She was hooked, devouring everything she could, then launching a business as a raw chocolatier. "I was good at what I did," she told me. "But, I got bored, I learned everything I could, and the mind-numbing repetition drove me mad. So, I ended the business."

This made perfect sense for Techla. For Mavens, once you've learned what you came to learn, it's time to move on. To non-Mavens, this often lands as being flaky or flighty. Ever the starter, never the finisher. How can you just keep starting things, then walking away? What these judgy non-Mavens are missing is that, for Mavens, it was never about the thing that learning led to; it was simply about the opportunity to learn.

Taming the shame.

Layered onto the potential to be labeled a dilettante when you bounce from one knowledge-well that's run dry to the next, Mavens may also feel a growing sense of shame around the lack of drive to "do" something with what they're learning beyond simply, well, learning it. Non-Mavens don't understand why you'd invest so much time and so many resources in something, unless you "put it to work." While learning, to non-Mavens, has little value beyond what you do with what you've discovered, for Mavens, the fact that the knowledge you've acquired has value to others is more a happy accident than a driving impulse. For you, it's more about the process than the application of discovery. That's okay. There's nothing wrong with you, and there's nothing wrong with being driven to learn for learning's sake. It's just the way you're wired. Once you understand this, shame begins to leave the building. You have language to not only understand why you do what you do, but also to explain to others what's really happening. Which brings us to an important realization.

Tapping your Shadow as a tool for learning.

Mavens often tap the work of their Shadow Sparketype as a learning modality, though they may not realize that's happening. Michael Karsouny (Maven/Maker) is a Lebanese painter living in New York City who creates massive, abstract paintings that radiate energy and color. You feel his work in your spine. But, for years, he felt a sense of unease, bordering on shame, about his craft. He's a painter who rarely paints. Michael spends only about 5 to 10 percent of his working hours applying paint to canvas or wood and any other medium. What gives?

When you hear someone is a painter, you might assume their Sparketype is that of the Maker, driven to create. Often, you'd be right. Not always. Remember, many Mavens are known by others (and come to see themselves) not for their love of learning, but for the act of creation or service it sometimes leads to. Michael, it turns out, is a Maven first, and a Maker second. The 90 to 95 percent of his productive time away from the canvas is spent researching and in contemplation. And, well, living.

He is a serious student of art, studying masters from nearly every era, school, and style, deconstructing their approaches, strokes, brushes, media, color blends, paints, ingredients, and philosophies. He takes his time, moving between aggressive consumption, observation, and quiet, lingering reflection and integration. It's all learning to him. When he does step into his studio to paint, he moves with stunning speed, drawing upon the vast wellspring of wisdom he's amassed as it bursts forth in an explosion of expression.

Still, he shared with me that, even awakening to this, he felt a lingering sense of guilt or shame. He is a painter; he should be painting. That's what painters do. I proposed a reframe. What if, for you, painting was not just an expressive act? What if it wasn't just your Maker impulse coming through? What if, in addition, the act of painting was your version of a living laboratory, where you get to take all you've studied and learned and use the paint to continue to test your ideas and theories and insights, but in a physical, rather than intellectual, way? The penny dropped. "Yes," he replied. "So simple. Paradigm shift."

Discovering he was a Maven/Maker, with the Maven taking the lead, was a powerful awakening for Michael. It allowed him to forgive himself. Painters paint, he'd been taught. The truth is more nuanced. Makers who paint, paint to paint. Mavens who paint, paint to learn. Maven/Makers do both, but understanding which is in service of the other is the difference between shame and grace.

How introversion and extroversion affect Mavens.

The way Mavens learn is often tied to their social orientation. Extroverted Mavens often turn to people, classes, and experiences to learn, though they'll revert to less interactive forms of learning if they can't find easy access to the living sources they find most valuable. Introverted Mavens, on the other hand, often turn to information, self-experimentation, research, more intimate learning experiences, and forms of "inner learning" like contemplation, meditation, and journaling, as well as media. If forced, they'll take a class. With lots of humans. Grudgingly.

Here's the challenge with this. Mavens are already so internally gratified by process, their learning quests can take them toward isolation. Throw in social wiring that leans toward introversion and you can end up an extremely well-informed, socially isolated, and deeply lonely hermit. Creating structures that serve as circuit breakers to pull you out of this wise-and-alone spiral can be important.

WHAT TRIPS YOU UP.

Like every Sparketype, Mavens tend to grapple with a fairly universal set of experiences that can lead them to a dark place. Certain things trip them up more often and more readily than other types. For Mavens, if you're not learning, you're dying. Anything that gets in the way of learning, or stops the process, keeps you from expressing who you are and doing the thing that sparks you. At the same time, because the impulse that drives Mavens is so focused on process and, often, that process can unfold in an all-consuming, solitary way, Mavens are also subject to broader challenges that create tension in the way they live their lives, the people they're in relationships with, and how they interact with the world. Let's start with one of the most prevalent triggers.

Trapped in a learning void.

In the early head-spinning days of any pursuit, for Mavens, there is generally a lot to learn, from discrete knowledge about a topic, field, or area of expertise to the culture, mission, and social dynamic of an organization. But here's the strange thing. While those fueled by other Sparketypes may be happiest once the "new information overload dust" settles, Mavens tend not to be. Why? Because Mavens gotta learn.

These experiences often hit a crisis point when, months or years in, Mavens find themselves in a position where there's little left to learn. Or so they think (more on this in the "Spark Your Work" chapter). For Mavens, this is death. They feel trapped. This is especially the case when they're a bit further into life, they've built a certain lifestyle, taken on certain responsibilities, and the only obvious way to kick-start the learning process is to disrupt everything and take a chance on a new position, organization, or industry. Where do you go from there? How do you get Sparked again? There are two ways to find out.

- One, understand you are a Maven. You must be learning or you're dying. Own the fact that learning is your work oxygen. Often, this simple acknowledgment creates a shift that leads you to start seeing and creating opportunities. Reimagine your current work. What might you do, even if it lies outside the confines of your job, that would unlock the learning gates for you?
- Two, reframe what your job is about. If it is "okay," provides a certain desired flexibility, financial security, freedom, and opportunity, but no matter how you try, just won't give you what you need on a learning level, what if you looked at it a bit differently? What if you saw it as more of a funding engine for your ability to embrace fascinating new learning opportunities on the side? Not to make money, but simply to spend more time growing?

Either one of these approaches can flip the learning switch back on and reawaken your Maven impulse on a level that makes you come back to life.

The black hole of obsession.

Because the Maven tends to be more internally focused, Mavens can find themselves falling into a bit of a learning black hole. They become so absorbed in the quest for knowledge that they ignore everyone and everything in their life that lies outside that process. If the well of wisdom or subject area that trips your learning desire wire is bottomless, that can lead to a work life that feels endlessly rewarding, but a life outside of work that more or less ceases to exist.

The risk grows when the body of knowledge that is the focus of a Maven's fascination is so vast, complex, and constantly changing or growing that it could take many lifetimes to master, if ever. The more aware a Maven becomes of the vastness of what is knowable, compared to what they know, the more irresistible the compulsion. They ignore self-care, relationships, and other nourishing experiences that are critical for physical and mental well-being. Maybe they're able to sustain this pattern for a while, but it always comes back to haunt them. When their vitality and connection buckets run dry, they will not only grind a Maven's happiness and well-being to a halt, they'll also stop them from working on a level that lets them fully express their Sparketype and their potential.

Because of this risk, it's important for Mavens to establish circuit breakers to help them know when it's time to pull out of the fascination-obsession abyss. Here are some examples:

- Create daily, weekly, or monthly check-ins with friends, family, or colleagues who know your impulse, understand its value, but are also empowered by you to call a time-out.

- Commit to participating in certain activities, clubs, leagues, societies, associations, gatherings, or other experiences that meet on a regular, scheduled basis.

Remember, a life of the mind is a vast and beautiful branch on the tree of a life well lived, but it's not the tree.

Lack of control.

Once a Maven latches onto a topic, it's game on. They often want to devour whatever wisdom is available. Anything that stops them from this pursuit doesn't just stop them from learning, it effectively stops them from living. When pursuing personal fascinations, this tends to be less of an issue, but in the realm of a career, it can become an issue. It generally is at its most painful point when you're early in your professional life. You have a certain amount of control over your time and resources, but are almost always working within the larger constraints and culture that set limits on your freedom to go all in. This can be incredibly frustrating, especially when you believe the thing you seek to learn will be immensely helpful to the bigger goal, vision, or outcome of the team or organization.

In these situations, some Mavens will take up the learning quest on their own time, not because they have to, or because they are getting paid to, but because they don't want their pursuit of discovery to be constrained by the limitations of some other person, team, or organization. If they're not given control to fully express their impulse "on the clock," they'll create their own clock that exists outside the confines of anyone else's rules. While, in certain contexts, this is seen as taking initiative and may even help some Mavens "get ahead," it can also appear as being politically motivated or pandering, isolate you from colleagues, and steal time from personal relationships and pursuits, which may end up causing rifts.

Other more rules-based Mavens may settle for doing what they can with the time and resources they've been given. This can help from a culture and team-player standpoint, but it may leave you feeling incredibly stifled, frustrated, and unfulfilled over time. Regardless of your tendency, know that this dynamic exists, and be on alert. Understand that it is most often experienced in the early days of work and, with time, you'll likely accumulate enough credibility, social currency, and control to be able to not just choose the areas to unleash your learning impulse, but also do it in a way that allows you more control over the process as well.

SHOW ME THE MONEY.

Tapping your Shadow to fund your Maven's learning impulse.

One of the blessings of the Maven is that it is the most internally gratified Sparketype. You can vanish into your learning cave and be entirely fulfilled, even if nothing of value to others ever comes out of it. But that can be a bit challenging if you also want to turn your Maven-ness into your living. I love the way Wayne Nelson (Maven/Scientist), from our Sparketype community, put it:

"My life in general as an unfocused Maven is pretty one-sided. Everything goes in. Nothing comes out. I am like a black hole of intellect. Rarely does feudal Japanese architecture, the history of money, the geography of Cuba, or whatever random bit of info I currently find interesting help me solve a problem or produce something. I do pretty well when I watch *Jeopardy*, but that doesn't pay the bills."

This is why Mavens often turn to their Shadow Sparketypes as conduits to cash, or as a "funding mechanism" for their Maven impulse. Neil Pasricha, the wandering bundle of curiosity you met earlier, is also an international bestselling author of books like *The Book of Awesome*, *The Happiness Equation*, *You Are Awesome*, and many others. His books and talks are meticulously crafted, deeply vulnerable, and generous expressions of his Maker Shadow, and also highly effective mechanisms to fund his life and his continued ability to spend inordinate amounts of time learning.

Teaming with others to transform insight into income.

Another pattern you'll often see with Mavens who seek to earn a living from their impulse is a reliance on others to unlock the economic value of the knowledge they accumulate. This is why Mavens often function well on teams, where they play the role of domain expert, contributing to the collective efforts of others who then apply that expertise to the creation of a product, service, idea, or outcome that becomes the source of compensation.

The tension between money and Mavens.

While leveraging the work of your Sparketype as both a living laboratory and a source of income can be a powerful way to come alive (and live well), there's also potential hidden risk. The pursuit of the "value creation for others" side of things can become so all-consuming, it takes you out of the pursuit of the pure quest for knowledge that, for the Maven, makes the entire thing worth doing in the first place.

So much energy often shifts from the pursuit of learning to creating the thing learning enables that others start to see and identify you, first and foremost, as the artist, the entrepreneur, the teacher, the coach, rather than the Maven. Everyone starts telling you who you are in their eyes, and you start to mistakenly accept that imposed identity as your own. You spend all your time doing the work of your Shadow Sparketype because it's the identity you've assumed—more for convenience and belonging than anything else. This leaves you with less time for pure learning and you start wondering why, instead of coming alive, you're dying inside. It's because you're suppressing your Primary Sparketype.

William Brown (Maven/Sage) could blissfully lose hours, days, months, even years learning. For years, he was a technology consultant, specializing in audiovisual technology and installations. In the early days, the consulting funded both his quest to learn about the field and its applications and his life, so he kept expanding it. He built a 13,000-square-foot technology center and quickly found himself mired in the plate-spinning overwhelm and anxiety of being a small business owner. Not only was William's venture no longer supporting his deeper love of learning, it'd all but annihilated the time and emotional bandwidth needed to research and learn about the tech-driven topics that called him.

Eventually, he decided to wind down the business. As he sat in solitude and began to create the space he'd all but removed from his life, he started to revive.

William's Maven impulse returned, this time focused on the very thing he'd struggled so mightily with over the previous years and, in many ways, for his entire life: how he identified himself. That grew quickly into a fascination with understanding how people identify themselves, then build lives around those identities. A new learning quest was set in motion. And, to support it, he decided to build a living laboratory—but this time, in a very different, gentler, and more sustainable way that centered on learning, not business.

He began coaching, then launched the daily *Disconnect to Connect* web-show on Facebook. There, he would spend the better part of an hour with a single guest exploring their lens on identity, through the vehicle of a single word they most associate with. This format lets William leverage his Sage Shadow (drive to teach) to build an audience and platform to teach others, which is capable of eventually generating income and also serving as the living laboratory that fuels his Maven impulse. Even better, he's doing it in a way that keeps his Maven side central and allows the rest to be in service of it, rather that losing himself to it.

THE
MAKER

You, in a Nutshell.

SLOGAN.
I make ideas manifest.

Animating impulse.

Makers gotta make. Creation is your call; it's the thing that gets you out of bed in the morning. You are most alive and engaged when you start with an idea, then turn it into something that exists in the world. Something that reflects the taste, sensibility, and notion of possibility you have in your head, the vision of what could be. And, now . . . it is. Because of you. Physical, digital, experiential, ethereal, or permanent, it doesn't matter (though some Makers are, in fact, drawn to specific channels of expression as we'll see), as long as you are making. Even if it's brutally hard, you know you're doing the thing you're here to do.

Makers are very heavily driven and also satisfied by process. When you are working in a way that allows you to spend the greatest amount of time immersed in the process of creation, you feel most alive. When the thing you are making is a true reflection of your vision, your unique ideas, lens, values, and sense of taste, you become Sparked. When you have control over the resources, steps, decisions, and ultimate vision and are in charge of all of the elements that allow you to work toward that idea you see in your mind's eye and know is possible, you come alive.

Max.

Growing up in Colorado, Max Levi Frieder (Maker/Nurturer) found an outlet from his earliest days in nearly any form of creative expression. Deeply passionate about family, friends, and the outdoors, he had no lack of love for people and life. But when he'd draw or paint, he'd lose time. It called to him, and Max knew at a young age he was a Maker, even though he may have associated more with the medium than the impulse. But that would all change as he entered adulthood.

Max earned a spot at the legendary Rhode Island School of Design where he studied painting and largely assumed he'd become a fine artist. Upon graduating, he started down that road but then a left turn led him to a summer job facilitating collaborative painting projects with teens and he came alive on a whole different level. His Shadow Nurturer worked in a fascinating bidirectional way. It allowed him to coordinate creative experiences that let kids feel included, valued, confident, and expressed—while also generating a wellspring of input into his creative process and vision.

Max was Sparked, and he turned his infectious energy toward a much bigger, collaborative art vision. He began to organize and facilitate large-scale, outdoor collaborative art projects, where he invited kids from the local community to come and create with him. The feeling of creating was always his more joyful place, but this newer experience of creating in a collective way and knowing the work was helping others express their own creative impulses, while also serving as a conduit for trauma and a channel for storytelling, took the experience to an entirely different level. His co-makers, where he goes, are not just local artists and facilitators, but a community of kids in some of the most challenging circumstances, from underresourced neighborhoods in the United States to refugee camps in war-torn countries.

Max eventually joined with a partner, Joel Bergner, to cofound Artolution, a foundation with a mission to seed and facilitate large-scale, outdoor collaborative art projects, help kids share their stories, and also serve as a vehicle for other, often underresourced, artists and teachers to step into their own place of expression. Artolution, itself, has become a new way for Max to express his Maker impulse, as he works with a team to build an organization, a community, and a set of protocols that allow the vision to create a perpetual ripple in the lives of displaced children and families around the world.

Different domains.

Interestingly, when most people think about the process of creation, of building something, they think in three dimensions and physical materials. Homes, painted canvases, furnishings, art, books, and so on. But it doesn't have to be that way. Especially in the increasingly experiential and digital world in which we live. What you make may be a physical thing, but it could also be an experience or an interaction. It could be digital, words, numbers, code, apps, or programs. It might be a moment, work of music, event, company, business venture, or anything else. You may find yourself drawn to specific tasks, tools, topics, or media along the way, but the deeper, innate impulse to make is still the essential driver of your effort.

The Maker also happens to be my Primary Sparketype; my Shadow is the Scientist. As a kid, I'd beg my parents to drive me down to the town dump on a Sunday morning, where I'd scavenge bike parts, bring them home, vanish into the garage, and duct-tape them into Franken-bikes. Over the years, Franken-bikes morphed into painting when I discovered my grandfather's old paint set. Experiments on canvas grew into album covers on jean jackets, painting and then renovating houses, essays and books, letterpress printing, building companies, brands, designing websites, and hundreds of other pursuits. The through line for me, the red thread, has always been the process of creation, taking an idea, teasing it out, and making it real. Few things make me happier than when I'm in my Creation Cave, whether that looks like an art studio, a notebook computer, an adult summer camp, or a printshop.

Early and often.

More than many of the other Sparketypes, the Maker impulse tends to reveal itself early in life and without much effort. Reason being, it's not only socially acceptable to devote time to the process of creation, it is often encouraged and rewarded. Family activities, classrooms, and workshops are devoted to the process. Teachers work it, in some way, into nearly every topic. Studying history? Make a diorama. Learning about cells? Let's build a 3D cell together. We don't have to go out of our way to find opportunities to make things. They are all around us all the time, from our earliest days.

Laura.

Laura Peña (Maker/Advocate) is an animator, designer, and film-maker. Growing up in the Dominican Republic, she was always drawing. Everyone around her thought she'd become a fine artist. But her mind was more drawn to creating physical spaces. She'd vanish into a room for hours, moving boxes and pretty much anything else she could find to create physical representations of imagined environments. In her mind, the box in the corner would be an oasis in a desert. She was moving people around, creating scenes, and telling their stories in virtual space.

Laura eventually moved to New York to study design at Parsons School of Design. After graduating, she began building her career at an agency designing video games for kids, before focusing on digital motion design for everything from TV to film and the online realm. What started as designing and creating physical spaces in her childhood home for imaginary characters to move through evolved into a career building entire virtual domains, beings, and stories for millions to enjoy. But the virtual world wasn't enough.

Eventually, Laura's Advocate Shadow Sparketype began calling her to apply her creative skills to make something that was more meaningful to her. To create in a more purposeful and heart-centered way. It gave direction to her Maker impulse.

As a young girl in the Dominican Republic, she'd benefited greatly from those who recognized and encouraged her to pursue what made her come alive. Laura was passionate about helping young girls discover and nurture their own uniqueness, so she decided to tap her Maker skills to create a visual experience that would amplify the voices of girls around the world and help

MAKER

them claim their own power and stories. She launched the She Is the Universe movement (sheistheuniverse.org), became a one-woman film crew, and began traveling the world interviewing teenage girls and featuring them in three- to five-minute mini-docs. And, of course, she designed and built the She Is the Universe website and not only films, but also produces, edits, and creates the motion graphics and special effects along the way. It's amazing to see how that early Maker impulse to create spaces and tell stories has evolved and danced with her Advocate Shadow to create new ways to express itself over a period of decades.

The vision/ability gap.

There is a phenomenon that shows up often in the earlier journeys of Makers that legendary public radio producer and founder of *This American Life*, Ira Glass, describes as the gap between taste and ability. You can see, in your mind's eye, what you want to create. You're developing a sense of style, a voice, a set of preferences and ideas. A certain creative sensibility. You know what you want the thing you create to look like, feel like, sound like. You know the story you want it to tell. But you haven't yet acquired the technical skill or mastery to be able to express it. And you know, deep down, it may well take years, or decades. Maybe, you begin to wonder, it'll just never come. This experience can be astonishingly frustrating. It knocks so many people out of the path of creation, not because they don't have the capacity to do great work, but because they don't have the patience and the will to stay in it long enough to close the gap between their mind's eye and the thing it yearned to make real.

As a young painter, I struggled mightily with this. I knew what I wanted to paint, but couldn't make it happen. As a young guitar player, I heard the melodies and riffs in my head, but could not make them come out of my instrument. Craft and vision have their own timelines. Makers who become extraordinary in any given domain are very often the ones who stay in the game long enough for both to evolve to a place where they can finally dance to the same tune. If you are a Maker and you're feeling that seemingly never-ending level of expressive discontent, know this—there is nothing wrong with you. Nor are you doing the wrong thing. It's just part of the process. The only way to close the gap is to stay on the path—to keep creating long enough for your ability to rise to a level that is capable of making manifest what you hear and see and feel in your Maker soul.

WHAT TRIPS YOU UP.

While certain circumstances allow you to come fully alive, others shut you down. These are your triggers. They tend to exist within certain circumstances I call Danger Zones. When you get triggered, you tend to go "Dark Side." It's important to know what your triggers, Danger Zones, and Dark Sides are, so you can anticipate them and, if possible, make decisions that allow you to avoid them and pre-plan your workarounds and recovery strategies in advance.

Because you're not a bot, but rather a living, breathing human with a heart and a brain and a unique set of life circumstances, your triggers, Danger Zones, and Dark Sides will be unique. Still, here are a few that tend to arise more often in the lives of Makers. Let's start off with what I call the three quirks of the Maker.

The three quirks.

- Quirk 1: Boredom with systems and scale. You may well find yourself losing interest the moment the making/hyper-creation element of any endeavor fades. The moment things become stable or systems-based, you get antsy. Even if it's something big, cool, interesting, and impressive. Something you "couldn't wait to begin." Once a project moves into more of a stable-growth phase, you need to figure out how to stay largely in creation/ideation mode or you're onto the next thing.
- Quirk 2: Disconnection from output. Another oddity, you may find yourself in love with the process of building something, but also oddly emotionally disconnected from the final "thing." Not because it didn't matter, not because you don't love it, but because it was the process that held the truest experience of purpose, expression, and meaning for you, not the product.
- Quirk 3: Disconnection from impact. Your creations may have a tremendous impact on others. You may invent a product, create art, build an experience, brand, or company that delivers everything from joy to salvation. What you make may well change lives, shift conversations, elevate communities or colleagues. You enjoy knowing this. But when you're really being honest, as good as it might feel, it's not

the essential reason you do it. The fact that it moves people, and the depth of that effect, is more a measuring stick of your capabilities and ability to fully express your vision and impulse than it is a primary motivator for effort.

———

Collaboration in creation.

Decision by committee, followed by creation by committee, can be the bane of your existence, especially when those involved have different values, visions, and sensibilities. For Makers, with a strong sense of identity tied to a specific idea or ideal of what the process and outcome should look like, being constrained, hindered, or having your vision diluted by the input of others can be incredibly frustrating.

Healthy, well-aligned, and harmonized collaboration is great, but it often works better when each person has their own "creation domain" within a larger context or project. Or when there is a clear and agreed-upon "lead Maker" who largely sets the vision and approach, then brings in others to make it real. Being forced to share decision-making over parts of the process related to your unique vision, lens, and taste can become highly triggering. When you create with others, you may struggle with any scenario that requires you to work over a long window of time as part of a group, where you do not have substantial control over the decisions that are important to you and allow the work to be the most direct expression of you, your voice, lens, and vision.

Also, frequent, formal meetings that require presentation, negotiation, and resolution with others who have a substantial say in the outcome can be pretty triggering. When forced into these situations, you can feel frustration, anger, withdrawal, disillusionment, and dilution. While everyone has a different dark side reaction, for Makers, it's not uncommon to either withdraw from the process or project or, if you don't have the power or leverage to stand your ground, accept the possibility that your vision will be diluted and complete the job, while feeling like you've left a bit of your soul on the cutting room floor and stopped contributing on a level that let you come alive.

HOW TO MAKE IT WORK FOR YOU.

For young Makers, especially, who work in a larger group or collaborative context but don't yet have enough clout, credibility, or power, it's important to choose carefully, negotiate wisely, and be clear about where your line in the creation sand is. Get a clear understanding of what the decision-making process will be for any endeavor before you say yes to it. Suss out who holds power and leverage and how malleable that dynamic is. Integrate this into your decision to launch or join a project, team, or organization. Eyes wide open always. And be very clear about your vision, contribution, power, and control going in, so that surprises are kept to a minimum.

At the same time, understand that making anything substantial may well require you to involve others in the process. And while their input may challenge or differ from yours, if you hold yourself open to it, be deliberate and considerate, rather than reactive, you may well find yourself opening to their ideas and more capable of making something that might be different from your original vision, but also better.

Resource constraints.

Similarly, having little control over the resources needed to make the thing you're working on, or not having enough control over the process of what you are working toward, can be incredibly frustrating. It forces you to constantly step out of the fiercely generative creation flow you so love in order to spend time in "admin" mode. For Makers, that's about as much fun as eating sand. Endeavors that are either underresourced, rely on outside contributions that are not responsive to your needs on a timely basis, or where you lack power/leverage in a scenario, coupled with substantial responsibility to deliver on a promised outcome, can feel impossible. When this happens, you often shut down. What to do? Seek information about the process, resource availability, funding, access, and control in advance. If certain things require you to rely on outside resources, be proactive about expectations, timing, and availability. When possible, negotiate and agree to specifics in advance.

Beyond that, you might also explore a bit of a reframe. In the domain of creation, there is a universal rule. Constraint, annoying as is may be at first, breeds creativity and innovation. Explore the invitation to think differently, to envision and create differently in the face of limitations you may not have asked for, yet have become your reality. Frame it as a beautiful creative challenge to make at an even higher level, starting with even less. The beautiful thing with this reframe is that it not only pulls you out of a state of frustration, but when you *do* end up making something amazing, knowing that it came from an even more constrained, less-resourced place makes the process and outcome feel that much more rewarding.

Black hole of creation.

Because the Maker lies pretty far over on the process-satisfied side of the Satisfaction Spectrum (see appendix) and tends to be more internally focused, Makers can find themselves falling into a bit of a creation black hole. You become so absorbed in the process of making that you ignore everyone and everything in your life that lies outside that process. You end up doing good work, but also destroying much of the rest of your life in the name of making at your highest level.

If you ignore self-care as well, you can end up negatively impacting both your physical and mental well-being. When your vitality and connection buckets run dry, they will both grind your happiness and well-being to a halt and stop you from working on a level that lets you fully express your Sparketype and your potential.

Be on alert. Any circumstance that holds the potential for you to spend large amounts of time either alone or with people who are equally committed to your endeavor and willing to give up almost every other meaningful part of life in the name of getting it done can be intoxicating, and also devastating. Cultures and organizations that actively foster this approach to work, rather than providing alternative values, structure, and expectations, are danger zones.

Set up circuit breakers or weekly check-in mechanisms to help ensure that you are not just doing the work of your Sparketype, but also zooming the lens out and doing what's necessary to take care of your health, state of mind, and relationships along the way. Along with this, commit to and schedule specific "bigger life" moments, rituals, and habits, like exercise, meditation, relationship time, nature time, planned random nothingness time. The point is, the best time to set up the things that'll

MAKER

keep you from vanishing into a black hole of creation is before you take your first step in. The next best time is now.

Stay alert, be aware and proactive. If you find yourself in a scenario that is a potential trigger, respond to it quickly and, even better, do what you can to protect against sliding into your dark side long before it even happens.

SHOW ME THE MONEY.

Makers have a sometimes-complicated relationship with making, service, and money. On the one hand, it's a beautiful thing when you can sell what you make, be compensated on a level that sustains you, and not have to do anything else. On the other, you sometimes feel the pressure of making what you know will sell (or earn an income), rather than what you're called to create. It's always a bit of a dance. There is no universally right answer beyond the balance that makes you feel fully expressed, while also comfortably sustained.

Joel.

Growing up in the Bronx in the eighties and nineties, writer, musician, and performer Joel Leon (Maker/Maven) found both a creative outlet and a place of refuge in art. At five, he'd steal away, lost in his own world, writing, drawing comics, and free-style rapping in his mom's bedroom. "Hood kid, semi-poor kid, creative kid, artsy kid," was how he described himself in an essay entitled "Hip-Hop as Disruption," "straddling both bullet and book like balance beam ballerina."

Fueled by a love of hip-hop, writing, and performing, Joel earned a spot at New York City's iconic School of Performing Arts. He was good onstage and a regular at local rap ciphers, where poetry bound to beats landed as powerful freestyle. But underneath the performer, which often presented as his public persona, a deeper Maker impulse kept taking the wheel. Writing was always at the heart of his impulse. An unrelenting desire to create language and tell stories that laid bare the truth. Joel's Maven Shadow led him to study the work of so many writers of stories, social commentary, justice, and equity that had come before him. Both because he loved and was inspired by their work, but also because they brought him deeper into the craft.

Heading further into life, becoming a father and feeling the call to balance his Maker impulse with his desire to provide for his family, Joel embraced a blended path that is fairly common among Makers. By day, he's a copywriter, working on creative teams in the advertising and marketing world. He enjoys it. He's great at it. He gets to tell stories and work with great collaborators, while effectively funding his ability to not only live well and take care of his family, but to spend time in his alternate Maker mode as a public storyteller, writer, and author.

In that domain, Joel writes and publishes essays, poems, articles, and books that speak to everything from racial justice and representation in the creative world to reimagining parenting, mental health, music, and the craft of language. Each creative outlet informs and supports the other. Together, they create the scaffolding and the channels that allow Joel's Maker impulse to find its way into the world, make meaning, and leave him feeling seen, heard, secure, and alive.

While many Makers find a sweet spot with the blended approach, other Makers may earn their living not by selling what they create, but by guiding others in the process of creation. This can be incredibly rewarding, especially when your Shadow is the Sage or Advisor or one of the more service-driven, outwardly satisfied Sparketypes. Your Maker impulse satisfies the desire to turn ideas into things, but the process of doing what you do has value to others, so you share it in the form of anything from a course or class to workshops, mentoring, and more. This can be a very rewarding blend. But it can also create a certain tension.

Kristin.

A longtime member of our Good Life Project community, Kristin Livelsberger (Maker/Advisor) is a full-time art teacher. Kristin described her job as a bit of a push-pull. "Although I'm an art teacher, a seemingly amazing fit for a Maker/Advisor," she shared, "I find myself unsatisfied. I don't get to do much 'making . . .' I'm still working on how to 'tweak' my job to include more making, but crave a deeper desire now to create more with my garden and include on-site/in-garden workshops or sanctuary garden advisory services!"

This is a common refrain. Makers love to make. And they tend to dislike anything that pulls them out of making, even if they enjoy those other things or people that pull them away. There's always an underlying yearning to get back into the creative cave, and a sense of sustained low-grade grief that accompanies their inability to do so. It's neither a voluntary reaction, nor a judgment about the people or experiences that draw them away from making.

For Makers, the yearning to fully express their impulse and also honor a deeply held value of financial security may lead to the Maker's blend. Zoom the lens out and be intentional about where the line is for you. You may well find a way to earn as much as you need through your Maker impulse, especially over time as your level of craft and mastery allows you to express yourself at higher and higher levels. You may decide that unfettered expression is more important than compensation. You may

find a sweet spot in the blended path. You might find complementary outlets for your Maker impulse. That's what Kristin did,
focusing on an out-of-the-classroom creative domain, garden-
ing. No matter your choice, the more honest and intentional you
are, the easier it is to create the blend you need to feel Sparked.
We'll explore this in detail in the later "Spark Your Work" chapter.

MAKER

THE
SCIENTIST

You, in a Nutshell.

I figure things out.

Animating impulse.

Scientists are all about the pursuit of burning questions, wicked problems, puzzles, riddles, and quandaries. The more involved and complex, the better. You also tend to be very process-driven. Sure, solving the puzzle, finding the solution, or figuring out the answer feels great, especially if it ends up helping others in a way that matters to you. But it's the hunt, the process of discovery—or what Richard Feynman, Nobel Prize–winning physicist, described as "the pleasure of finding the thing out, the kick in the discovery"—that is equally, if not more, enlivening. You feel a sense of excitement, energy, and purpose not only when you arrive at an answer, but through the simple experience of searching for it.

When the question, problem, or puzzle you are pursuing is tied to an area, topic, person, or community you feel some personal connection to, or innate pull toward, even if you have no idea why it feels so compelling, you become even more drawn to the work and the feeling may well rise to the level of not just a devotion, but a calling.

Part of the process of problem-solving is also problem-identification, especially for Scientists who tend to walk through life seeing things in need of figuring out everywhere they look (which would be nearly every Scientist). Cultivating the ability to identify the problems that matter most to you and that you believe are most capable of being solved lets you focus your efforts on getting to an answer, rather than drilling a thousand simultaneous burning question wells and never having time to find answers to any.

Another part is about working, thinking, and acting in the space of the unknown, often when the stakes are high and people don't see things the way you do. Many Scientists, in fact, have a certain irreverence for the status quo that sometimes rises to the level of disdain for the current state of ideas, fixes, answers, and solutions. In the Scientist's mind, even well-answered questions are ripe for better solutions and answers that are just waiting to be discovered by them.

Aviva.

From as early as she can remember, Dr. Aviva Romm (Scientist/ Maven) has been fueled by a burning desire to figure things out. As a young child, she was constantly doing jigsaw puzzles, word problems, even cracking open rocks to see what was inside them. "I am that person," she shared. "If you are stuck on a desert island and you need to figure out how to get off or where to get the food, or where to find something, I have an intrinsic systematic way of thinking." This impulse to figure things out and come up with answers drove her efforts in school, science fairs, even primary school spelling bees where she'd deconstruct words into phonemes to figure out the meaning. Not because she had to, or even because she wanted the prize, but because the process is what made her come alive. It sparked her and, decades later, it remains a central motivator for action in all parts of her life.

Sitting on a couch, watching TV with her husband, she'll start googling things that come up in shows to help her better understand what she's seeing on the screen, then start trying to figure out what's going on at a deeper level. She's constantly scanning the horizon, in nearly every interaction with the world, asking why things are done the way they're done, followed almost immediately by "what if we did it this way instead?"

In her professional life, Aviva's Scientist impulse found a decades-long outlet and channel for expression in her work first as a midwife and herbalist, then as a physician, teacher, and leading voice in the world of functional medicine. She's the person so many women go to when they've been to everyone else, tried all the treatments, yet are left wanting and, too often, ill and dismissed. Her Maven Shadow has fueled decades of fierce knowledge acquisition. Basic familiarity isn't enough. She needs to be encyclopedic in her domain. Bundled with years of working with clients, patients, and colleagues, and a relentless desire to not surrender to the often-limited answers, paradigms, and approaches that have preceded her, she pursues and discovers new insights, ideas, solutions, protocols, and treatments that deliver results in cases that seem intractable and unsolvable to others.

This has meant, at times, bucking not only convention, but the entire lineage and culture of traditional medicine and the corresponding set of limitations, constraints, assumptions, and structures. All in the name of not only helping patients find a way back to health, but also redefining the paradigm of medicine for all, and bringing not just hope, but healing, back into the equation.

Aviva has found the sweet spot between her Scientist's impulse to solve, her Maven Shadow's impulse to know, and her innate desire to serve women in a way that not only allows them to recover, but also to reclaim a sense of agency and understanding. Work, for her, may be hard, really hard at times, but because it makes her come alive, it feels more like a calling than a simple way to earn a living. Aviva is one Sparked human.

A Scientist by any other name is still a Scientist.

There's a moment in M. Night Shyamalan's 1999 blockbuster movie, *The Sixth Sense*, where a young Haley Joel Osment, playing a boy who talks to the deceased, turns to Bruce Willis's character and says, "I see dead people." Scientists are the same, except, instead of dead people, everywhere they look, they see things in need of figuring out. Though, interesting enough, they're not always aware this compulsion underlies so many of their decisions and actions. For some, like Aviva, the impulse reveals itself in a very overt way early in life. For others, it's a central driver, but remains semi-hidden until experience and awareness bring it to the surface; then, once revealed, it takes center stage.

Alex.

Alex Hart (Scientist/Maker) was a fifteen-year-old, ninety-pound powerlifter growing up in West Texas. She was relentless in her pursuit of heavier and heavier weight, and fiercely accomplished at a young age. Like Feynman, attention and accolades were quick to come. She was "succeeding" by everyone else's measures. For her, it wasn't the weights she cared about. Or what the pursuit of lifting did to her strength, size, or appearance. It was the puzzle she was solving. Alex was tapping her Scientist impulse, using her body as a living laboratory. Powerlifting was the "physicalization" of the scientific process. Her results, simply data from a series of experiments others saw as "training," were her way of proving or disproving her hypotheses about what worked and what didn't. While everyone around her saw the pursuit of athletic accomplishment, strength, mass, and tone, for her, it was an almost entirely intellectual activity. Still, Alex hadn't yet seen this experience for what it was, the early hint at her animating impulse.

Alex eventually left lifting behind, but her Scientist impulse to find new problems and figure them out began to blossom. She went on to pursue law as a career—plenty of problems to solve in that domain—yet the field wasn't calling her. She wasn't interested in the nature of problems on offer. So, three years in, she walked away, got on a plane and flew halfway around the world, joined ed-tech firm Mindvalley in Malaysia, and worked on a team that would develop a chart-topping meditation app.

With the app launched, and that "thing figured out," Alex started looking for her next puzzle to solve. She returned to Austin, Texas, where she'd spend the next few years, taking on different business-development and marketing projects, eventually launching her own venture, Good Joo Joo, a boutique marketing and strategic growth agency.

Finally coming into her Scientist impulse to identify problems, solve them, then move on, Alex rapidly scaled up Good Joo Joo, and she and her team became known as a tactical and strategic strike force. They'd immerse themselves in complex rapid-growth puzzles, devise strategies, test, iterate, and optimize all in the name of figuring out what worked best. Once done,

SCIENTIST

they'd move on to the next puzzle. Just as a scientist might do in a lab.

Alex eventually created her own space to embrace the process that makes her come alive, choose the areas of focus that are of most interest, and handpick her collaborators. But there was something else going on. Starting her own company also gave her cover from a certain amount of social judgment that often follows the Scientist Sparketype who is called to follow a wide range of problems.

The Scientist shame game.

Some Scientists find themselves having landed in a field or with a focus that is so big and complex, so laden with endless sub-questions and problems and puzzles to solve, they can easily spend years on a single question or move seamlessly from one to another and still be perceived by the outside world as building a "coherent career." A cancer researcher may fully express their Scientist Sparketype through work in a single lab, diving deep into a single question or a series of questions over a lifetime. To the outside world, however, they're researching cancer. It's one thing. This provides a certain amount of perceived stability, grounding, growth, and the perception of "having direction and stick-to-it-edness."

Others, though, find themselves pursuing burning questions in a very different way, sometimes feeling judgment from those who don't quite understand the choices they're making.

Bob.

Returning to San Francisco after teaching English in Japan for six years, Bob Gower (Scientist/Essentialist) found himself working at the *San Francisco Examiner* newspaper doing layout and production. Every day was a new visual puzzle to solve. He moved up quickly, becoming design director before leaving to work on the design teams of a few dot-coms, then going back to school to get an MBA in sustainable business.

There, he became fascinated with how humans live and work and create in a sustainable, complementary way, and how organizations play their part. He immersed himself in organizational theories and methodologies, from agile development to holacracy, to chaos and complexity theory. So many problems, big, thorny puzzles. He was captivated by the possible avenues to exercise his Scientist impulse. He eventually found himself in the world of Silicon Valley tech, becoming a product manager, then an agile consultant for two startups, a management consultant, a writer, a facilitator of tough conversations at the highest level of enterprise.

He kept bouncing from domain to domain, problem to problem, all the while accumulating experience, wisdom, and honing his "figure it out" chops. From the outside, looking in, though, Bob appeared to be perpetually in flux. Blink once, different company. Twice, different title. Thrice, different industry. That's not how you build a career, people might think as they cast raised eyebrows. Especially those who are unaware of the Scientist impulse.

Compounded by issues of self-worth from the time he was young, Bob's seeming inability to "stick with one thing, one area, one company" landed as rejection and judgment from the outside-in, and shame from the inside-out. Alex shared a similar experience. It wasn't until both understood their sustained, primal through line—their Scientist's impulse to find new problems and puzzles to solve—that they began a process of understanding and self-forgiveness. The benefit of time has also allowed both to see the red thread that weaves through so many of their choices over so many years and find greater self-acceptance in their approaches to doing the thing that makes them come alive. Interestingly, they both tie back to a similar ethos, helping people and organizations figure out how to grow and create impact in a sustainable, healthy way.

Both Bob and Alex effectively built shields from social judgment around their efforts by creating their own containers for their pursuit of answers. Alex created Good Joo Joo, as well as a number of additional ventures. Bob eventually built his own practice and brand that gave him the cover of "Bob Gower, Consultant, Author, and Speaker," within which he created the freedom to pursue any number of experiments, burning questions, and puzzles.

Even if you don't know your through line up front, invariably, if you keep following the call to answer burning questions, you'll look back, years or decades from now, and not only realize you've done good work, but also be able to see with the clarity of hindsight how your choices have woven together a tapestry of problems and solutions that relate back to a common theme. If you don't find an easy home for your Scientist impulse under some other person's or organization's broad umbrella, that's okay. Give yourself the time and grace to figure it out, to move freely from problem to solution across any number of domains and entities. Hold your commitment to express your deeper truth tightly, and the expectations of those who might not understand your approach lightly.

It's personal, until it's not . . . and then it is again.

Often, Scientists are drawn to solving problems they have experienced themselves. What begins as a desire to scratch their own itch expands into something bigger, then inevitably comes full circle.

Rev. angel.

Rev. angel Kyodo williams (Scientist/Maven) is the second Black woman to be recognized as a *sensei* or teacher in the Zen Buddhist tradition. Rev. angel, as those in her orbit often refer to her, likes to color outside the lines. Has since she was a kid. A Black, queer woman growing up in the U.S. in the nineties, Rev. angel endured a lifetime of bullying, racism, sexism, exclusion, and oppression that showed up in nearly every way and every day. That experience led her on a quest to seek not just solace, not just justice, but answers. Ideas, practices, and processes that might, in some way, let her better understand how to free herself, breathe more easily, and understand the world around her.

Rev. angel discovered a set of tools, practices, and processes of inquiry, investigation, and revelation in the study of Zen, informed at every step by her own grounded sensibility and practical experience. Embracing her Scientist impulse, she found herself increasingly guided into deeper, more complex questions. That led her to devote herself to the pursuit of questions so many run from. The ultimate problem she sought to solve? Liberation.

For over two decades, Rev. angel has turned her fierce compassion, wisdom, and desire to seek and speak often uncomfortable truths on the intersection between systems of oppression and systems of liberation. Social justice, the dismantling of racism, and the embrace of freedom is, to her, not only about societal change, it's about personal liberation and reclamation. In her words, "race, love, and liberation." They are all intertwined.

Rev. angel's "scientific method" integrates a wide range of ideas, skills, technologies of living, and group-work with the goal of ending systemic, personal, and interpersonal oppression. She then shares her findings and invitations in everything from teachings and conversations to books, like *Radical Dharma: Talking Race, Love & Liberation.* Her ultimate goal—the problem she's devoted decades to solving—in her words, is to initiate profound healing and dismantle oppression across lines of race, class, gender, sexual orientation, and other divides. What started as a deeply personal problem expanded out into something societal, then guided Rev. angel back to the realization that systems don't change until people do.

WHAT TRIPS YOU UP.

Just like every other Sparketype, Scientists are prone to certain circumstances that hold the potential to trigger them and take them to a dark place. It's not about whether you've done something wrong. There are simply certain qualities of every Sparketype that tend to make you more or less susceptible to certain circumstances taking you out of balance and, instead of filling you up, emptying you out. The great news is, the more aware you are of these potential triggers, the better prepared you'll be to see them coming and avert them. And, if you find yourself spinning in one of these stuck-experiences, you'll better understand what's really happening and how best to explore the experience and take action to move back into a healthier, more constructive, and alive place. Interestingly enough, the triggers for Scientists are the exact opposite of what triggers so many other Sparketypes.

SCIENTIST

Certainty.

The air that Scientists breathe is the unknown. It's that place where something's not quite right and there's a better way out there, but what exactly that is, well, it's anyone's guess. Uncertainty is the soil in which they plant their seeds and grow their solutions. It represents possibility. As they work their Scientist magic, over time, answers start to come, solutions take form, and what was once the great unknown starts to come into focus. A specific, certain answer emerges.

While this is the end-state we're taught to spend our lives working toward, Scientists love the process of getting there, and they love the fact that they figured the thing out. But they don't love being there. It's highly unusual to find a true Scientist lingering or reveling in their solution. Instead, they're thrilled for a moment, then the impulse kicks back in and they're off to the next problem, dropping back into the realm of the unknown.

But what if there is no next problem? What if you're locked into a job, role, industry, set of processes, course-of-dealing, or context where everything is fairly figured out, nobody seeks change, and most people want everything to stay the same? If there is no next problem to solve or thing to figure, fix, or improve, you can't get lost in the process of figuring the thing out. You can't do the thing you're here to do if it has already been done, and no one wants it done better.

In an odd way, while most others yearn for certainty, security, and sameness, that same experience can become a growing trigger for the Scientist. If they dwell in it for too long, they get intensely uninterested, frustrated, and maybe even a tad cranky. They lose the ability to come alive and, instead, find themselves trapped in the process and slowly flatlining.

Martin.

For Scientists, the stifling nature of the locked-down life can show up in nearly any domain. Martin Nocchi (Scientist/Advisor) served as a priest for nearly fifteen years. He loved the experience of counseling parishioners and the challenge of creating and presenting moving sermons and assumed that would be enough. This would be his life. Yet, as the years passed, a growing discontent began to build. He wasn't entirely sure what was going on, but he knew what he felt.

Instead of deepening into his chosen path, he felt increasingly disconnected from it, even stifled by it. Over time, Martin came to realize the source of his growing emptiness. While there was a fairly regular stream of people, situations, and challenges to figure out, many were repetitions of the same patterns and problems that required the same advice. More, those moments represented a relatively small part of his work. The vast majority of his waking hours were spent in routine, prescribed ritual, systems, and repetition.

For many, this would be desired, even comforting. Especially in service of others. But for many Scientists, including Martin, who are innately fueled by novelty, uncertainty, possibility, and process, the weight of the perpetual sameness became stifling. So much that he decided to do something others might consider a bit radical. He left the priesthood to pursue another path.

Seeking counseling from mentors within the church before making his decision, he was asked, "What about your faith?" For him, he replied, leaving to find a way to contribute to others by finding or creating a path that honored, then built around his intrinsic drive to live in the question, and spend vastly more time devoted to solving problems, was a greater act of faith than staying. He wasn't abandoning God, he was finding a different way to connect and serve that also allowed him to contribute from a more authentic, alive place.

For the Scientist, the simple truth, the one that seems almost unfathomable to so many who are wired differently, is that being able to perpetually traverse the path from uncertainty to certainty is where you come most alive. When things become too known, too routine, too locked down, when you are not in pursuit of questions, problems, answers, and solutions, you begin to wither on the vine. If you're a Scientist and you're feeling the malaise of a devotion, path, or career that leaves little room or need for living in the question, explore how you might either expand or shift your work, or the way you do it, in order to step back into a question that is interesting enough to trigger your impulse toward effort.

Lack of control.

Control is often a major sticking point for Scientists—or, more accurately, lack of control over the process of inquiry and the resources needed to pursue the solution you seek. Collaborative inquiry, working with a team, can be a powerful experience, when the team is balanced and the approach of each person is complementary. But, when team members approach a problem differently from you, and they have some level of control over the process, things can get tense quickly. Shared control and collective decision-making and action-taking can be agony for many people. For Scientists, with a strong sense of identity tied to a specific idea or ideal of what the process and outcome should look like, being bound to, hindered, or having your quest and process diluted or interfered with by the input of others can be incredibly frustrating.

At the same time, there can be incredible benefit in the ability to harness the collective brainpower and potential cross-pollination of ideas and insights of multiple people. Understand that pursuing answers to anything substantial may well require you to involve others in the process, and while their input may challenge or differ from yours, if you hold yourself open to it, be deliberate and considerate, rather than reactive, you may find yourself opening to their ideas and more capable of embracing approaches or finding solutions that might be different from your original vision, but also better. The net result may well be a certain amount of surrender over the process, but the ability to get to a better outcome.

Lack of training in the alchemy of fear.

While living in the question is the place that holds the greatest opportunity for the Scientist, it is also the place that can hold the greatest destructive potential for personal well-being. It's a bit of a double-edged sword. The way you are wired requires you to wade into uncertainty to do the thing you're here to do, but that doesn't mean you are emotionally or psychologically equipped to flourish there, let alone survive. Especially when the stakes are high, even life-and-death.

Most people, Scientists included, experience high-stakes un-certainty as anywhere from mildly discomfiting to emotionally brutal. For many, fear, anxiety, and doubt become a persistent bedfellow. Beyond making you feel awful, an elevated level of anxiety has a secondary and equally damaging effect. It stifles creativity and problem-solving ability, especially insight-based problem-solving, which is the place where Scientists often find their biggest breakthroughs.

What to do, then? Similar to Makers, in order to not just survive, but thrive, Scientists must learn to transform fear into fuel. Learn and cultivate the skills, practices, and processes of the mind needed to find higher levels of equanimity and capability in the face of high-stakes uncertainty. Adapt to a more agile, iterative workstyle that "chunks" uncertainty and validates your hypotheses along the way, keeping the stakes at any one stage relatively low. Embrace physical and mindset practices, from meditation and breathing exercises to movement, that give you increasing access to equanimity and stillness, even in the midst of the pursuit of answers to big, complex problems where the stakes feel unbearable. Understanding this dynamic and cultivating these skills was, in fact, the sole focus of my book *Uncertainty: Turning Fear and Doubt into Fuel for Brilliance.*

SCIENTIST

Rabbit holes.

Because Scientists tend to be more internally focused, they can find themselves falling into a bit of a burning-question black hole. You become so absorbed in the quest for answers that you ignore everyone and everything in your life that lies outside that process. You end up doing good work, but also destroying much of the rest of your life in the name of finding a solution.

The risk becomes higher when the burning question, problem, or puzzle that is the focus of your quest is so vast, complex, time-constrained, or personal that it could well take many lifetimes to figure out.

This may create a certain time pressure to work harder and longer in order to get closer to solving all that is solvable in whatever time you have. It can lead to obsessive-compulsive, almost addictive devotion of your waking hours in the name of getting there faster. Without adopting the lens of possibility and gratitude, the level of consuming obsession can become a futile and destructive quest. It can leave you not inspired and grateful, but dejected, demoralized, and so burned out and estranged from everything else that made your life good, you're no longer even capable of effectively solving the problem anymore. You may be able to sustain this pattern for a while, but it always comes back to haunt you.

When your vitality and connection buckets run dry, they will not only grind your happiness and well-being to a halt, they will also stop you from working on a level that lets you fully express your Sparketype and your potential. Similar to other Sparke-types who are driven by a consuming and process-focused effort, it's important to create practices that allow you to thrive and circuit breakers that tell you when your pursuit has become unhealthy and even unhelpful, so that you can hit *pause* and do what's necessary to come back to a healthier place.

SHOW ME THE MONEY.

Scientists have an "interesting" relationship with money. In the world of business or work, there are really only two ways to get paid. Deliver a delight or solve a problem. The latter approach is what the vast majority of businesses and jobs center around. The bigger the problem and the deeper the pain, the greater the potential payoff and the higher the potential compensation. Not always, but often. Because of this, Scientists tend to find themselves in demand and well paid, especially in domains where the stakes are high and the impact is vast. Scientists tends to be one of the Sparketypes that find the easiest and broadest potential for full expression and meaningful compensation in work and life. Classical roles in research or science are low-hanging fruit, but as we've seen, the impulse can and often is in full bloom in an incredible array of fields, industries, and titles.

That said, when Scientists find themselves innately drawn to a problem, question, or puzzle that is of deep interest to them and maybe even to society, but offers no clear, predefined path to income or economic value to others, they may find themselves torn. They struggle to make a choice between the pursuit of a burning question, especially one that aligns with either personal relevance or an area of innate interest, and either their own value of financial integrity or the expectation that they "be responsible" by those whose approval they seek.

In order to resolve this tension, similar to other heavily process-fueled Sparketypes, like the Maker and Maven, Scientists may find themselves pursuing more of a blended path. They'll earn a living through work that both taps and financially rewards their impulse to solve, albeit in an area that is not of great interest, then unleash that same impulse "on the side" in relation to problems or questions that may not provide meaningful financial compensation, but do strongly interest them. More on this approach in the "Spark Your Work" chapter.

The beauty of the Scientist impulse when it comes to the question of earning a living is that the world is an unending maze of questions and problems. With a little bit of effort, it's nearly always possible to find or create whatever opportunities you need to both harness your impulse and also sustain yourself in the world.

THE
ESSENTIALIST
You, in a Nutshell.

SLOGAN.
I create order from chaos.

———

Animating impulse.

For Essentialists, the impulse is all about order, distillation, simplification, and clarity. Because order—and not just anyone's order but rather your unique approach to it—is a primal driver of effort. But also because, for many Essentialists, usefulness and beauty (even if they don't use those words) are important values, and your brain sees order as the foundation of both. When everything is in its right place and presented in a way that just makes sense for the Essentialist, so, too, does the world. It doesn't matter where you go, whether at work or home or on vacation (or a restaurant, store, experience, etc.), Essentialists see chaos, mess, complexity, lack of organization and, instead of wanting to cry (like me), it triggers an urge to create order and simplicity.

Essentialists also tend to think in systems and processes, with the goal of sense and sensibility. Interestingly, because they are often very process-driven, the end result of their work may well deliver extraordinary benefit to those around them, and that's great. Essentialists enjoy knowing the fruits of their labor are making a difference in the work and lives of others. And delivering results or outcomes may be pegged to how they're rewarded or compensated. But it's often not their primary *why*. It's not the main reason they do what they do. The praise and gratitude and even income that often comes along with it is simply one way for them to measure how successful and skillful they've become at the process. It's the opportunity to immerse themselves in the process that truly makes them come alive.

When the challenge you are working through is a true reflection of your vision, your unique ideas, lens, values, interests, and sense of order, you become Sparked. When the domain or field or topic area is something you're intrinsically drawn to, you become Sparked. When you have control over the process, resources, and vision and are in charge of all, you become Sparked. And, most important, when you complete the quest and you can step back and see the transformation, that is massively fulfilling. Then, like most other process-fueled Sparketypes, you're on to the next project.

Jenny.

Walk into Jenny Blake's (Essentialist/Maven) living room and the first thing you see is a wall of books. First thought, "Wow, that's a lot of books!" Then it hits you: there's something else going on. Every book on every shelf is ordered in a particular way. Not by author or title. Not by Dewey decimal. Not by fiction or nonfiction or genre. Every single one is arranged by the color of its cover, in the sequence of the rainbow.

Red fades to orange, which eases into yellow, then green, gently morphing into blues, then indigos, finally delivering you a dozen feet down and to the right into the violets. Of course, a special place is set aside for the black-to-white spectrum, which is a healthy part of her canon.

First impulse . . . run! This could only have been done by the mind of someone with serious issues.

Second impulse . . . fascination.

How, I wonder, does Jenny's brain work? What would motivate a human being to do this with over a thousand books, and then maintain it? Before I get my answer, the other shoe drops. As I stand before the wall-o-books, half-wondering whether to head for the door, or pull a book out, ease it into a different spot, and see what wrathful response awaits, Jenny takes me deeper into the elegance of her system. "It starts with color," she says, "but do you notice anything else?" A beat passes. Hmmm, nope. "Height," she responds. "First is color, then height, then topic. I honestly don't understand why anyone would do it any other way."

Jenny's living room library is just one of many ways her Essentialist impulse shows up in a personal way. This same impulse has driven incredible outcomes in her professional life as well. It fueled top grades in college, where her notes were so organized, she ended up turning note-taking into a paid side-hustle for other students. Upon graduating, her systems-and-processes approach to making things clear and getting things done served as the driving force that landed her a position in one of the biggest tech companies in the world, where she quickly started rising up the ranks.

That same impulse then led her to reimagine the often chaotic, nonlinear, and frenetic way so many people develop their careers, devising frameworks, tools, systems, and processes that helped simplify and add clarity to the process of career development and transition and birth two bestselling books, *Life After College* and

Pivot. Yearning to claim a fuller sense of control over the way she earned her living and also her ability to build and offer tools that helped others simplify and "sensify" the choices they made in work and life, she eventually went out on her own as a consultant, author, and speaker where she could fully embody her Essentialist nature.

Essentialists on teams.

When it comes to teams, Essentialists are often not only the sanity-makers and progress-enablers, they're the glue that holds the ship together, especially when the seas get stormy. While most others run from complexity and chaos, hoping someone else will figure it out, Essentialists run to it, and turn it into workable systems and simplicity that allows other team members to breathe easier and get more done.

Lindsey.

Lindsey Fox (Essentialist/Nurturer) has been a part of our work family for years, starting as a general process-whisperer and eventually becoming a podcast producer. For five years, we gathered our Good Life Project community for a three-and-a-half day, four-hundred-plus person adult summer camp. Lindsey built the processes, systems, spreadsheets, checklists, and operational backbone to keep the madness and ever-expanding volume of moving pieces humming.

As the *Good Life Project* podcast began to take off, and our live programming went on hiatus, Lindsey merged her love of process with her deep connection to audio programming, eventually becoming the show's producer. Over a period of years, her Essentialist impulse shifted focus to evolve with her interests and our needs. She built out and manages the complex and dynamic process needed to keep more than forty episodes in various stages of production, from booking to publication, at any given time. I love creating the podcast. Crafting the container for intimate, revelatory conversation about the experiences and insights that make people come alive makes me come alive. My time in conversation with so many leading voices and luminaries enriches my life in countless ways. None of that would be possible without my Essentialist partner-in-impact wrangling the perpetual cacophony of moving pieces, noise, chaos, and complexity that defines the behind-the-scenes reality of any established media platform. Important as it is to my ability to do what I do, the thought of building out the entire production process gives me hives. For Lindsey, while it's not always easy, it's the thing that animates her. Essentialists, it turns out, are very often not just the glue that holds everything together, but the process-makers that turn dysfunction and paralysis into function and progress.

———

Essentialists are indispensable.

Essentialists not only create order from chaos, they develop, sustain, and evolve the very processes and systems that do everything from creating harmony, clarity, insight, and spaciousness, to more effectively and efficiently driving outcomes and growth. For that reason, alone, they tend to be highly sought after and, once found, pretty indispensable. Yet, there's a second, even more visceral reason for their indispensability. The work of the Essentialist is also unique in a way that is very different from the work of most other Sparketypes. How? It's often outright loathed by every person who is not wired the same way.

For years, I did not believe Essentialists existed. Their wiring is so contrary to mine, I could not conceive of anyone being innately called to step into the eye of a tornado and begin the arduous and meticulous process of pulling down information, action-steps, resources, documents, items, inventory, data-points, ideas, and beyond; assess their value and position; then build systems, structures, and processes that make it all accessible to others. That type of work leaves me wanting to curl up in a ball and binge-watch every season of *Grey's Anatomy*! Twice. Turns out, I'm not alone.

The vast majority of Sparketypes not only share different impulses for effort, they also share a disdain for the very work Essentialists can't get enough of. And, because that work is also perpetually in demand and highly valued, the person who does it masterfully will always have a place in any number of endeavors, teams, or projects. Essentialists are not just essential, they're indispensable. Not only because they *can* and *want to* do what so many others cannot, not only because they are catalysts for clarity, progress, and growth, but because Essentialists save all the non-Essentialists from having to do the important, yet unimaginable work themselves. This very blessing, however, can sometimes become a curse. More on this in the "What Trips You Up" section below.

It's not a quirk, it's what you do.

Interestingly, while others tend to recognize the work of the Essentialist early on, Essentialists themselves can sometimes be a bit blind to it, until some experience or observation, often by someone other than them, brings it front and center. They think,

"Organizing, distilling and simplifying isn't *what* I do, it's just the *way* I do everything."

Monisha.

Considering herself a "people person," Monisha Rahemtulla (Essentialist/Nurturer) started her career in human resources. She liked helping people and volunteered often as a kid, so she figured it would be a good fit. Working in recruiting, she spent her days helping people find jobs, working on their resumes and searches.

On the surface, the service element should have been deeply rewarding, and it was, especially to her Nurturer Shadow. Still, something was missing. She began to realize the part of the job she enjoyed most was gathering and organizing information, distilling it down on people's resumes to help them tell a compelling story. She often looked at that not as a primary skill or form of contribution—it was just the way she approached her job.

Monisha shared her feelings with her father-in-law, who suggested looking into the related field of compensation and benefits as a specialization, since it was a high-demand area. She had no idea what compensation and benefits was, but she was excited about the opportunity to do something that centered her Essentialist drive, rather than treated it as a fringe player in her work life. She quickly discovered the field had an intense focus on number crunching, data analysis, and managing projects. It was all about distilling, ordering, and simplifying as a way to extract meaning. Essentialist work. It was a light-bulb moment.

Recognizing her ability to organize information and draw the story out of the numbers, Monisha's managers worked with her to develop this competency, bringing her more opportunities and increasingly complex, high-profile projects. She realized she could stay in her chosen profession but devote herself to a specialization that immersed her in the systems, processes, distillation, and insight extraction that made her come alive. It wasn't just the way she did things, it was what she did. Who she was. As I write this, Monisha has been doing this for more than twenty-five years.

WHAT TRIPS YOU UP.

Just like every other Sparketype, Essentialists have their Achilles' heels. There are certain danger zones—circumstances, experiences, interactions, and expressions of their impulse—that can lead them into a dark space. Once there, unhappiness, discontent, and dysfunction can start to set in. It's important to have a sense for not only these general triggers, but also the subset that you, personally, find yourself more at risk of. We explore the main ones here, as a way to help recognize them, so that you can more readily see them coming, take action to avoid them, and find ways to short-circuit the patterns and head in a more constructive and positive direction—even once you're in their grip.

The Essentialist's Curse.

Ever hear the phrase "if you want something done, give it to a busy person"? Well, Essentialists often suffer from a similar perception. Because of it, they may endure a crushing level of demand for the work they do. Essentialists' work is not only central to the success of nearly any endeavor, it's also the work most others dislike and are relatively bad at doing. That can lead to scenarios where non-Essentialists, especially ones with some level of control and power, consistently hand off work they could—and likely, should—be doing to the nearest Essentialist. Once the Essentialist does a good job, and they generally do because it's the work that makes them come alive, everyone else takes notice. Accolades and recognition come, but along with that comes an awareness of your ninja skills by more and more people who also want you to do their Essentialist work. Yay, them. Not so yay, you.

The ripple created by your unique impulse and abilities leads to more recognition, advancement, and opportunity, coupled with exponentially more people and projects discovering you, and wanting to give you more work than you can handle. Eventually, you fold under the pressure of everyone else's asks or, worse, just give up and leave. If you find this happening, it's critical to understand that the firehose of work will never stop until you create and enforce boundaries that allow you to breathe again—and also devote yourself to the projects you say *yes* to on a level that allows you to revel in the knowledge that you're able to do your best work. Learn to see your impulse and abilities as a blessing. You will always be in demand, but also know that with that blessing comes a responsibility to define who, how, when, and why you'll say *yes* to work.

Essentialism by committee.

Essentialists often struggle when people, especially those without a similar sensibility, get in their way. For them, order-making by committee or lack of control over the process and resources that allow them to distill, simplify, and make meaning can feel anywhere from mildly annoying to downright crushing. Sure, this tends to be tough for most people. For Essentialists, with a strong sense of identity tied to a specific idea of what both the outcome and also the process should look like, it's not only an annoyance, but a refutation of their identity and value.

Being tied to a process that is created by someone else or, what more often happens in the world of work, by some collective decision-making team or body can feel stifling and emptying. The deeper into a project they get, the worse the problem feels. Every bit of labor invested in a process or working toward an outcome they believe is less efficient, intelligent, or effective than their approach feels like work wasted, time wasted, life-force drained. And, by the way, this is not just about a person's job; it often rears its head in personal lives as well.

Control vs. dominance.

Early in his career, Koesemanto Bong (Essentialist/Sage), or "Koes" as everyone calls him, started out as a software engineer. His Essentialist nature led him to spend time not just writing code that did the job, but also automating steps that were toilsome, continually reworking code to be more efficient, and cleaning up confusing logic, making it easier for everyone else to understand. Elegance mattered as much as endpoints.

Rising into leadership as an engineering manager, that same impulse found an outlet in the creation of processes and optimizations that helped to make work and life easier for everyone. In that context, his Essentialist nature was appreciated and rewarded. But, as with most Essentialists, that same impulse can sometimes get in the way in other parts of life. With his characteristic smile that makes everyone around him join in, Koes shares, "I am all about efficiency, sometimes driving my family crazy—from making sure our calendar events are in order, to creating a spreadsheet for our vacation, to optimizing dish-washer space so we can load and unload as easy as possible."

Monisha offered a similar reflection, sharing how her family chides her when they go camping. As the Essentialist mom in charge, she has a methodical and elaborately organized system of setting up the campsite. She knows exactly how it needs to be done, but can't describe it to anyone else. When they try to help, it's like they're getting in her way, so she shoos them away and insists on doing it herself, her way. In the case of Koes and Monisha, the quirky need to be in control leads to more laughter than anguish, but that's not always the case, especially in the context of work.

When we're talking about projects nobody else wants to take on, let alone lead, the Essentialist impulse to take charge is often ap-preciated. In the context of projects where those around you truly do want to participate, however, the impulse to define and control both the process and the outcome can cause strife. It effectively excludes others, often those you need, and may even make them feel unappreciated, dismissed, and devalued. Plus, in certain sce-narios, it's actually the mess, the chaos, the holding yourself open to the unknown where the greatest stories and adventures lie. So, it's a constant dance. In order to protect against this, keep asking:

- How much does it truly matter that I am in control in this specific context?
- Are there other, bigger priorities or concerns that might take precedence over my need to control the process at this moment in time?
- Is my approach really so much "better" that it justifies my push to control?

All of this brings us to one of the root triggers for Essentialists.

ESSENTIALIST

Efficiency vs. effectiveness.

For Essentialists, efficiency is often their metric for assessing success in both developing their process and in the outcomes they create. They're constantly looking at the experience to simplify, remove steps, streamline, and distill. If they can find a way to get to the same place as someone else with less effort, complexity, stress, and waste and with fewer tangents and redirects, that is the ultimate aspiration.

Problem is, efficiency and effectiveness are not always — or even often — the same. The cleanest way to get something done isn't always the best way to get it done. Nor does it always lead to the optimal outcome. This is especially apparent in the process of innovation and creativity. Innovation requires a certain amount of sustained mess. It is what's known as the divergent phase of the process, where the job is to take down the walls of the ideation container and let in everything, even the most off-the-wall inputs and ideas.

It's not only about allowing chaos, but rather calling it into the conversation. You know, up front, the vast majority of ideas will not be viable and will be thrown out. Still, if you avoid the mess and try to create a process that proceeds directly to the orderly "distill and validate" convergent side of creation, you may end up pushing through to a solution or product or offering more efficiently, but the likelihood that it represents the true capacity of the people involved is pretty slim. You not only need the mess, you need to stay in it long enough for first-order garbage to give way to second-order mediocrity, which then seeds third-order genius. Shut that process down in the name of efficiency and you may drive your team from point A to point B with greater speed, but what if the most powerful, transformative answer was point C, which lay at the end of a tangent you

ESSENTIALIST

were not willing to allow anyone to travel down, let alone acknowledge, because it was just too messy?

Interestingly, innovation methodologies have begun to emerge over the last decade that do a better job of accommodating this. Approaches like design thinking or human-centered design champion the need for early experimentation, ideation, and mess, but within the container of a well-thought-out, progressive process that leads eventually to focus, iteration, and production. These innovation operating systems can provide a great middle ground that gives Makers and ideators the freedom to do their thing, while giving Essentialists enough structure to breathe and know "their time is coming."

Compulsion and isolation.

As we've seen, the Essentialist's impulse to create order can sometimes rise to the level of extreme rigidity. That can cause friction with others. There is, in fact, a step beyond rigidity that can be more concerning, and that is compulsion and force. The quest to create order may, at times, push toward obsessive-compulsion to make everything perfect *and* keep it perfect and orderly, all day, every day. Piling on, because Essentialists tend to be more internally focused and process-gratified, they can find themselves falling into a bit of a simplify-and-organize black hole. They become so absorbed in the quest for order and control that they ignore everyone and everything in their lives that is outside that process. They end up doing good work, but also risk never truly rising into their potential because they were more concerned about order than evolution. And they simultaneously risk destroying much of the rest of their lives in the name of perfecting order.

The risk of this becomes higher when the challenge that is the focus of your quest is so vast, complex, and constantly changing or growing that it could take a huge effort and weeks, months, or even years to create the systems it needs. For this reason, it is important to have what I call circuit breakers and pattern-shakers. If you know you have this tendency, designate people in your work or life (or both) who know you and this tendency well and who you trust, then empower them to tell you when they're concerned that you're headed off the efficiency rails. Create time to listen, then agree upon future steps and possible changes in behavior to ensure you come back into a healthier place. Even if people aren't readily available to perform this role, create circuit-breaker moments attached to certain dedicated triggers, like a weekly or monthly check-in where you reflect on specified prompts that help broaden your lens a bit and discern whether it's time for a reset.

SHOW ME THE MONEY.

While the Essentialist impulse to create order, structure, simplicity, and clarity is valued and praised in many personal scenarios, from cleaning up your room as a kid to creating and sharing amazing notes and outlines as a student, it tends to be highly in demand in a professional setting. Within organizations, the work you do is mission-critical. Your efforts may play a key role in everything from making sense out of data and distilling information into usable insights to building processes and systems that allow nearly anything to happen. Essentialists are catalysts for insight, action-taking, efficiency, effectiveness, and outcomes. Because of this, you and the work you do will always be highly valued. Whether that value translates to income is another question.

When your Essentialist impulse finds an outlet in a domain or industry that assigns high economic value to what you do—think finance, IT, pharma, and many others—you'll likely find yourself not only indispensable, but also well compensated and sought after. You may, however, find yourself drawn to fields, causes, or pursuits that desperately need what you have to offer, and that you feel a strong affinity to, but also either don't place the same economic value on your work, or simply do not have a level of funding that allows for similar compensation to other industries. In those cases, you may well find yourself making intentional choices, based on how much you value full expression and financial security.

You may also find yourself exploring more of a blended path, which we dive into in more detail in the "Spark Your Work" chapter later in the book. Or, you may find yourself creating your own vehicle, often in the form of a private practice focused on anything from professional organizing to logistics and project management. This may be a satisfying approach to both earning a comfortable living and doing as much of the work that fills you as possible.

Regardless of the choices you make, remember, what you do is incredibly important, necessary, valued—and, in many fields, rare and indispensable. You are a unicorn. Own that, then do the work to find the sweet spot between how you choose to bring this impulse to the world, and how you want to sustain yourself.

THE
PERFORMER
You, in a Nutshell.

SLOGAN.

I turn moments into magic.

Animating impulse.

Performers come alive when animating, enlivening, and energizing—breathing life, emotion, and sensation into an experience, interaction, engagement, moment, role, or pursuit in a way that makes it come alive with energy, emotion, and understanding.

Performers are among the rarest and most misunderstood Sparketypes. Many bounce between feelings of shame when they go full-on Performer and repression when they stifle this impulse that family, friends, colleagues, and society in certain domains exalt and revere, yet in others, disdain and even punish. It is also one of the most misdirected Sparketypes, in no small part because it is so often artificially constrained by the notion that it can only be expressed in the world of the performing arts.

This is not only wrong, it's tragic. (I know, I know, so dramatic.) It denies Performers the opportunity to bring their impulse to bear in the exponentially larger landscape of possibilities with no obvious connection to the performing arts. Plus, it denies friends, families, colleagues, businesses, and communities the immense life-enlivening benefit that comes from being in the presence of a Performer who has been empowered to do their thing in full bloom.

Like all other Sparketypes, Performers tend to most fully access the feeling of being Sparked when the thing they are breathing life into is also a true reflection of a strong interest, vision, values, and a sense of taste.

Performers are unusual in that their ability to come fully alive integrates elements of both process and service. Many Performers derive great joy and satisfaction through the process side of things. They love the study, practice, and refinement of their craft, which often takes years to develop. Still, the ability to bring this impulse most fully to bear and become Sparked requires them, ultimately, to interact with others — or else they find themselves, eventually, performing into the void.

Author Kate DiCamillo once told me that, as a writer, the final act of creation is not when a book is published, but rather when a reader completes it. This applies even more so to the work of the Performer, because the fundamental nature of it requires the existence of and connection to other beings.

That begs the question, "What does it mean to be in relation to others in the context of performing?" Short answer: it's complicated. We live in a world where a performance can happen in real time (synchronous) or at different times (asynchronous), and the mode of engagement can range from intimate and in person to virtual and global:

- People in a theater watching actors onstage? That's real time, in person and semi-intimate.
- People in a boardroom interacting with a Performer facilitating a conversation? Real time, personal, and intimate.
- People at a bar watching a bartender put on a show? Real time, in person, and likely less intimate.
- What about people in a theater watching a movie, months after the performative work has been completed? That's asynchronous, remote, and mass-scale.
- What about students taking live remote classes? Synchronous, remote, and anywhere from intimate to mass-scale.
- What if the lessons are delivered in the form of prerecorded video that is viewed on demand at a later time? Asynchronous and remote, again, though given evolving technology that allows for the feeling of being in a virtual room, polling, chat, and visual feedback, things are getting a bit murkier.

Every Performer is unique in their preferences. There is no universal answer when it comes to the mode of engagement that allows Performers to most readily get what they need from an experience to fully come alive. The important thing is to understand that these things matter, often more than Performers realize. Some are fine doing their thing before a camera and knowing the final act of engagement, connection, and performance will happen months or even years later. Others are fine with a screen between them and the intended audience, but the experience doesn't give them what they need unless it's all happening in real time. Still others need to be in person, in a room, theater, going for a walk, or any other setting that "sets the scene" for the Performer to come alive.

Current video and audio platforms make this exponentially more accessible. If you're a Performer who is fortunate enough to be in a place where you get to do your Performer thing on a regular basis, but you're still feeling empty, look at the mode of engagement. You may well find a strong conflict there, which then gives you the road map to re-create your offerings in a way that is more likely to make the experience come alive both for others and for yourself.

Yvonne.

As a child, Yvonne Ator (Performer/Maker) found herself perpetually singing, playing music, and dancing, from family gatherings to local stages. As so often happens, over time, the impulse faded into the background as Yvonne stepped into adolescence, then adulthood and university where she was pointed away from her Performer's impulse and toward the practice of medicine. Funnily enough, Yvonne would have never applied to med school but for a random sign. On the last day of the application period, she stumbled upon an article about doctors who were also musicians. In the back of her mind, that would be her path. Once in med school, the consuming demands of her training hit. She tucked her Performer impulse away, focused on her studies, then began life as a physician. Sparketype impulses, however, can be stifled, but never extinguished.

Within a matter of years, a series of awakenings began calling Yvonne to leave the practice and devote herself to helping doctors survive the often crushing stress and burnout of the profession. While this new work felt more aligned with her passion for helping people flourish, something wasn't entirely right. Around this time, she'd decided to check out Camp GLP, an adult summer camp gathering our team at Good Life Project facilitated for five years. For the first time since her childhood, her Performer impulse found its way back to the surface. "Camp was like my yearly onetime performance," she shared, "but not just on the stage. Just by me being myself, for some reason, there was some kind of power that happened in my interactions that let me know that there was something else going on in terms of how I was showing up. . . . And I knew I was hiding. I'd been hiding for a long time." Discovering her Sparketype, so much made sense.

Yvonne began to explore what it would look like to harness her Performer impulse in the context of helping physicians thrive, with a focus on coaching, workshops, and retreats. She noticed that people were showing up not only for her insights, but for her presence, her ability to create a certain energy of safety and aliveness that opened them up, let them breathe again and feel more inspired, connected, and alive. Her Performer was in full bloom.

When the pandemic hit, with the pressure and stress on healthcare professionals amplified, Yvonne knew she'd need to shift the way she brought her essential nature to bear. She began offering weekly virtual respite sessions to give physicians a safe space to breathe, share, and be. Yvonne quickly realized the sessions served a dual purpose. The docs she was in service to continued to have an oasis to move through a brutally hard time, while also allowing her an outlet for her Performer impulse to breathe life into the moments and interactions in a way that made her feel most alive. "We were talking about really intense stuff," she shared. "I come off those calls and I could run a marathon. I just am like on fire. . . . And again, it wasn't about me."

Performers, it turns out, are all around us, even when they don't call themselves Performers. But they're also very often in hiding, until something happens that lets the impulse take center stage.

A lifetime of stifling—"If you've got it, hide it."

Performers sometimes hide their impulse, even deny its existence and convince themselves that their yearning to animate and enliven an experience isn't really at the heart of who they are. Three potential stigmas fuel this phenomenon:

- It feels too egocentric and self-centered (hey, world, look at MEEEE!!!!).
- It's culturally disapproved, not a socially appropriate way to be. Australians call this Tall Poppy Syndrome, though nearly every culture has its analog that says do not outshine those around you or draw excessive attention. Clearly, though, social media has become a powerful counter to this stigma.
- The only outlet is performing arts and, "oh, honey, that's a lovely hobby, you can do it on the side, but it's not an appropriate thing to pursue as a living, because, hey, you know we love you, but nobody you know— including you—makes it. And, you don't want to be living hand-to-mouth as a struggling artist your whole life. That's just not what responsible adults do."

This conditioning, at times, comes in subtle nods. Other times its overt to the point of being delivered like a daily truckload of bricks on the Performer's soul. The inevitable result, for so many, is to stifle the impulse—which leads Performers to potentially even deny its existence in the name of sidestepping judgment and shame. The cost of this repression, however, can be devastating, both emotionally and physically.

Jodi.

I met Jodi McGarahan (Performer/Advisor) backstage on the *Mel Robbins Show*. Mel was doing a segment on reimagining work in your fifties. Jodi was invited as a guest to share her experience and, to a certain extent, her struggles. I was there as a guest expert to brainstorm ideas. The night before arriving, Jodi had completed the Sparketype Assessment. Her Primary Sparketype was the Performer. But backstage, though we connected only briefly before going on air, something felt a bit off. She was quiet, a bit anxious and hesitant, withdrawn even. Not in an "I need to be in my special place before I go onstage" way, but rather in a quiet, somewhat defeated, stifled life-force kind of way.

As a kid, I'd learn, Jodi was obsessed with role-playing, acting, putting on shows, and singing. It's what lit her up. But, as her Performer impulse began to emerge in a more central way and she grew a bit older, her mother snuffed it out. She let Jodi know it was not an appropriate way to be, nor was it a worthy pursuit because she'd never be good enough to make it her living. What Jodi heard was, "The impulse cannot be valid if you can't rely on it to earn a living." Wanting to keep harmony in the family and feel the love and appreciation of her mom, Jodi walked away from her Performer impulse. She eventually pursued a career as a nurse, then a second act in business. She was very successful in both, but also never quite satisfied.

Sitting next to Jodi on Mel's show, I noted that, looking at her work history, I was surprised to see the Performer come up as her Primary Sparketype. I asked if there was something that she'd been keeping hidden inside. Yes, she replied, she'd loved performing her whole life but walked away from it. That's real, I offered. Her eyes welled. I felt the heaviness I'd seen backstage begin to lift.

Jodi had felt an overwhelming sense of sadness or loss her whole life. She had a beautiful family, a comfortable life, but knew, deep down, there was something missing. She had this yearning, but not for material things. When she took the Sparketype test, for the first time in her life, it all made sense. She knew she'd been hiding something that was so essential to her ability to flourish, it was time to let it out. "I was emancipated by the Sparketype test," she shared, "because I never would have understood why I was always craving something more. . . . The moment that I realized who I really was and came home, I started casting my net out there and seeing what I would find. So many things are happening. It's just amazing and I'm not afraid anymore."

It's a beautiful thing when shame leaves the building, and you open up to validating your innate impulse to invest effort in something that makes you come alive. Funnily enough, once Jodi reclaimed her inner-Performer, she was also able to recognize how it found ways to sneak out in her past careers: singing to patients as a nurse or putting on a show as a sales executive. In fact, the Performer impulse often finds its way out in ways that look nothing like what we'd assume were traditional domains for performance.

Beyond performing arts.

When we think of the Performer, we very often think about only the most traditional modes of expression—theater, film, singing, dancing, acting, spoken words, and similar genres. But when we talk about the Performer as Sparketype, we take a much broader lens.

It's not contained by a traditional channel or genre. It is about the call to engage with experiences, interactions, moments, opportunities, and people in a way that brings the interaction alive and infuses it with energy, emotion, and, often, connection and trust. It's about amplifying and animating nearly anything in a way that focuses attention, bypasses boredom, dances past defenses, enhances engagement and understanding, and lands in a more meaningful, impactful way. It's about giving moments energy and life.

The Performer can also easily thrive in roles that revolve around athletics, performance art, public speaking, comedy, facilitating business trainings, workshops, events, running meetings, teaching high schoolers, scooping ice cream, tending bar, leading a team or company, or nearly any other setting. The central feature is the impulse. The thing that lights you up more than any other part of the activities of the job is the performative/demonstrative aspect of whatever you do, and the reaction you get from those who are moved by what you've performed.

Erin.

Erin Bellard (Performer/Essentialist) grew up dancing. It was her everything. Encouraged by her parents and those around her to embrace the call, she pursued it as a profession and eventually earned a place as a dancer for the Houston Ballet. While the primary outlet for her Performer impulse came through dance and literal stages earlier in life, it found a very different path and a different, more metaphorical stage as her life and career evolved.

Erin eventually moved to New York City and, as so many who land in the city that never sleeps do, found work in the restaurant

PERFORMER

business. She saw a quick parallel between performing onstage and the type of theater that great hospitality called for. Erin intuitively got it. The front of the house, she realized, was all theater. It's why, in ballet, the entire troupe would devote months to rehearsal. Every little thing mattered. Same thing with world-class dining experiences.

Applying her Performer's impulse, work ethic, and commitment to craft in a different domain, Erin quickly rose up the ladder in the restaurant world, eventually joining the team at Crafted Hospitality, the restaurant group founded by renowned chef and restaurateur Tom Collichio.

There, she helped build out and launch one of their iconic fine-dining restaurants, where every element, from the food to the presentation, setting, music, service, and vibe, was designed to create drama. She describes the process like building a set for a show, hiring the backstage crew, and "casting" the front of the house to not just deliver food, but create extraordinary moments. This was great preparation for Erin's next big move, taking full control of the reins with the launch of her own place, e's bar, this time with a "set" built around the gritty, alive energy of legendary Lower East Side clubs of the seventies and eighties like CBGBs, The Mercury Lounge, and Max's Kansas City.

Walking into e's, you immediately notice thousands of band stickers plastered pretty much everywhere, as if put there by patrons over a period of decades. In fact, years in, many have been placed by patrons, but Erin personally selected, bought, and placed the original thousand or so to create the right backdrop for the community theater that unfolds on a nightly basis, with adoring regulars and newcomers joining the dedicated cast and audience. And, of course, Erin still loves not only owning the place, but also being one of the cast, playing her role in the energy and experience.

Size doesn't matter.

One of the common misunderstandings about Performers re-volves around the concept of an audience, what it is and is not. As we've seen from Erin's experience, an audience can exist in nearly any domain, not just performing arts. It can be thousands of people in a theater, dozens of diners in a restaurant, friends around a bonfire, colleagues in a meeting, or revelers in a bar. The size doesn't matter. It is about what happens between those engaged in the moment, experience, or interaction. In fact, it's even possible to bring your Performance impulse fully to bear before an audience of one.

Scotty.

Scotty Johnson (Performer/Warrior) grew up in Scotland. His given name, in fact, is not Scotty, but his heritage and accent led friends to start calling him Scotty and, well, the rest is history. While he loves being onstage playing his uke and telling stories, Scotty earns his living tapping his Performer impulse in a radi-cally different way.

For years, he's been bringing groups of people, from high school students to executive leadership teams, into extreme nat-ural environments from the Arctic Circle to the Oman Desert or the Amazon jungle. He handpicks the locations not just for their drama and ability to cultivate awe, but also because they organi-cally push the edge of physicality and emotion that sets the stage for connection and revelation. Once immersed in the location, Scotty meticulously guides his adventurers through a series of experiences, interactions, prompts, and conversations that ele-vate trust and lead to disclosure, vulnerability, and self-discovery.

These expeditions allow him to bring his Performer instinct to bear, but it was a brief moment with a single individual that best illustrates the purest expression of this instinct, along with the opportunity to tap it no matter how many, or few, are on the receiving end. Scotty was consulting with the leadership team of a large public company. The CEO was a powerful and intimidating person, with whom many struggled to be fully transparent. Scotty saw this dynamic unfold, recognized the tension it was causing and its potential impact on communications, morale, decision-making, and performance. He wondered how best to address it, spinning scenarios in his head. Finally, he decided to simply invite the CEO to go for a walk. While he couldn't bring the CEO into an extreme environment, he could create an outdoor experience that also involved physical movement to add a bit of a pattern interrupt, novelty, and drama.

Just like the best performers when they walk onstage in live theater, Scotty went through the same mental process he'd embrace prepping to step in front of an audience. Walking side by side near the Thames, he asked a simple opening question that he knew would quickly focus the CEO's attention, be provocative, but also be offered within a moving container of trust and intimacy: "What is your experience of receiving and listening to direct, honest, and constructive feedback?" He then stepped more fully into performance mode as he guided the conversation into tougher topics, enlivening and animating concepts and awakenings, drawing the CEO into a co-creative experience that came alive.

Ideas, insight, and even deeply challenging feedback entered the interaction in a way that bypassed the self-defensive impulse that would've, and had, ended the conversation when others had tried to broach similar topics. Scotty created a different context and a sense of power and honesty that engendered openness, energy, and receptivity.

Rather than blowing up, the CEO was transformed, much the same way an audience is transformed through the experience of breathtakingly honest and relevant theater. He was incredibly grateful, and that conversation led to a series of changes in behavior that then rippled through the executive team and, in turn, the organization. This is the power of a skilled Performer operating in a nontraditional domain. For Performers, it's not about the size of the audience, it's about the effect.

Tango, not solo: the power of the collective.

Very often, the work of the Performer is the work of collaboration. There is the interaction with the audience, whether one person, dozens, hundreds, or thousands. If you've even been to a Bruce Springsteen concert, you know this to be true. Attendees in the front rows on the floor by the stage bring signs with the names of songs. Bruce often steps up to the front of the stage and waves the signs forward, encouraging people to pass them up to him. He looks, then stacks them up to become a rough setlist for the show.

Throughout the often four-hour experience, he welcomes you into the music, just as a friend might welcome you into their home. Not just to listen, but to move, to chant, to close your eyes and vanish into the moment with him and the always alive E Street Band. At any given moment, he's singing to you, and you're singing back to him. You have this distinct experience of Bruce and the band not just being utterly in the moment with you, but also floating in the embrace of a sort of shared ethos of togetherness and hope. That sense of we're all in this together. As part of the experience, members of the audience, in effect, become co-creators in the performative act.

PREFORMER

There is a give-and-take at every step that either expands or constrains the experience.

At the same time, Performers often collaborate in a more structured way with their officially designated players. Actors work with other actors, musicians, directors, and crews. Speakers with other speakers, meeting organizers, planners, tech and stage crews. In organizations, leaders, colleagues, facilitators, managers, employees, and teammates most often work together, whether in preparation for or during a presentation.

A great performance is, almost always, a co-creative or collaborative act. Understanding this actually takes the pressure off a bit because "hey, it's not just about you." It's about the quality of the interaction, the setting, the context, the safety and trust and openness that allows all participants to step into the moment. It's not just a generative act, but a generous one. We're in the moment together. We create it together. We rise together. When that happens, especially at scale, there is nothing like it. It is transcendent.

WHAT TRIPS YOU UP.

Every Sparketype has its dark closet, triggers and places where work and life tend to go sideways. Performers are no different. Whether working to enliven and animate moments and experiences with others or alone, whether in a more traditional performative setting or a less conventional venue, similar issues arise. When they do, they not only stop the Performer from doing the work they do, they create a level of stifling and futility that, especially for Performers whose very expression depends on the ability to "let something out," can feel like a lead blanket on your work and life. It's important to understand the most common stumbling points, so you can hopefully see them coming and avoid them. When you can't avoid them, you will know when you're in them and in need of taking action or asking for help to get back on track. Here are the key triggers for most Performers to be aware of, avoid, and, if necessary, recover from.

Negative association.

On occasion, when people discover their Sparketype is the Performer, they'll reach out to me to share how they dislike the term *Performer*. I always ask why. The answer is universal. Performer, they've come to feel, is about being "a fake." Even worse, it's about playing up the drama to bring unwarranted attention to yourself. It's about wanting undue attention and praise.

The word *performative*, for some, denotes an act that professes to be done with benevolent intent, but in truth it is driven more by a self-serving desire to win points in the eyes of some group, community, or audience. Performative aid. Performative activism. Performative allyship. Performative posting on social media. Performative leadership. Performative sacrifice. Performative dog walking. Performative volunteering. You get the picture. Building on these associations, Performers may feel compelled to walk away from not only the word, but the work. This is not the answer.

All of these perceptions, in fact, can be true. But there's a deeper truth. The most effective Performers are not actually the ones who dial up the drama for the sole purpose of ego gratification, attention, and reaction or those who put on a facade. Rather, they're the ones who dial up the authenticity, integrity, trust, and craft in order to enliven an experience, moment, or interaction in a way that opens others to emotion, trust, connection, transference—and, at times, understanding, transcendence, even revelation. The intention is for the experience to land more as a gift that invites, connects, and elevates than a demand for adulation or adoration.

Think about the theatrical performances where you've been not just temporarily distracted from life, or marketed into giving your time to an insincere, self-congratulatory experience, but rather entranced, awakened, and deeply moved. Viola Davis in *Fences*. Robin Williams in *Good Will Hunting*. Awkwafina in *The Farewell*. Morgan Freeman in *The Shawshank Redemption*. Ben Platt in *Dear Evan Hanson*. Or Billy Porter in *Kinky Boots*. Think about Martin Luther King Jr.'s "I Have a Dream" speech, Jill Bolte Taylor's TED Talk, Maya Angelou's recitation of "And Still I Rise."

Think about Randy Pausch's famed Last Lecture, or the class or lecture or teacher whose ability to make nearly any topic come alive transforms the experience from rote transmission to full-contact awakening. My seventh-grade science teacher, Mr. Katz, opened class by grabbing an archer's compound bow and a toilet plunger, running to the back of the room, and firing the plunger over our heads and into the chalkboard up front. I loved seventh-grade science, not because I love science, but because I loved how he brought science to life.

Think about the global community of storytellers from the Amazon to Kathmandu to The Moth whose simple presence, voice, and words take you from laughter to tears, then leave you with a renewed sense of hope and insight. Two years ago, I sat in a theater, elbow-to-elbow with an audience of five hundred at the monthly Creative Mornings gathering in New York. SYPartners founder Keith Yamashita entered the room with a quiet grace. For the next hour and a half, against a curated soundscape, he relayed the story, often sitting in his chair, of his struggles and awakenings since experiencing a stroke a year before.

By the end, five hundred no-longer-strangers sat, hand in hand, many of us sobbing with recognition and gratitude.

Now, ask yourself a question. Do you view these people, their performances, or the way they make you feel and think about yourself and the world with a disdaining eye? Doubtful. In fact, these Performers and performances are revered not just for their skill, but also for their authenticity, mind- and heart-opening power, and generosity. For how they make us feel. When we talk about the Performer Sparketype and the work they're here to do, this is what we're talking about.

Turns out, it's not the work of the Performer that leads to the common misperception of fakery and self-centeredness, but rather the misplaced actions and intentions of a Performer whose pursuit of the impulse has gone a bit off the rails.

Rigidity.

Every performative act is, inevitably, also an act of co-creation. It is important to develop your craft, then rehearse and prepare thoroughly no matter the domain. Part of that process is about anticipating expectations and reactions, in the quest to cultivate energy and evoke emotion, trust, and understanding. Problem is, when the Performer rubber hits the road, reality almost never matches expectation. Which is why, for Performers, rigidity is death. For their intended audience and for them.

Paul.

Paul Sockett (Performer/Maven) has been a working actor for more than fifteen years. He describes the dance between allegiance to a source intention, plan, or script and the need to be responsive beautifully. When he takes on a role, he is effectively stepping into someone else's context. Their story, their characters, their script, their staging, their vision.

There is a certain amount of allegiance that is expected to those elements. Yet, he still feels a responsibility to hold any given performance lightly, to deliver on the vision of the producer, while also constantly scanning his fellow performers and the audience to ensure the way he brings his part of the experience to them lands in a way that feels alive and resonant. Because every night is different, he changes the way he delivers every night. A huge part of performing, Paul shared, is about listening with the intention of creating something that lets the audience say *yes* to going on the journey with them.

The real magic, it turns out, happens when you prepare intensely, then devote yourself to the craft on a level that allows you to let go of the script, talking points, or rigid agenda, focus your awareness outward, rather than inward, and give those around you what they need.

Lack of control.

Performers, especially as their craft and instincts develop, often yearn for control. Not just because they've "gotta be them," but because they may believe they can see a better way to bring an experience, moment, interaction, or role to life. Not having the power to do that, in their minds, hurts everyone. The truth may lie somewhere in the middle. There may well be ways to add performative elements, ideas, and insights that might raise the vibrance of the experience, but even the most experienced Performer isn't always right. In nontraditional performative domains and settings like heavily bureaucratic, regulated, or administrative settings, there may be very good reasons to dial back the performance in the name of legality or protection. Your Performer's instinct, deployed in a high-stakes government contract negotiation, may increase the likelihood of getting to *yes*, but it may also land you and your organization in regulatory hot water. Always beware the context.

Look for ways to step into a higher level of control and responsibility over the vision and process. At the same time, understand that making anything substantial may well require you to involve others in the process. While their input may challenge or differ from yours, if you hold yourself open to it, be deliberate and considerate, rather than reactive, you may find yourself opening to their ideas and more capable of creating an outcome that might be different from your original vision, but also better.

Mind your headspace.

Performers are unusual in that their satisfaction comes through a dynamic blend, from being heavily process/craft-driven and fulfilled to being strongly fueled and nourished by service and elevation, and everything in between. Obsessive commitment to either extreme can lead to a world of internal struggle. Focusing entirely on process can lead to mastery, but it can also send you into an obsessive spiral fueled by unhealthy levels of self-absorption, perfectionism, isolation, and self-judgment.

On the other side, obsessive focus on the audience can become equally defeating. You wind up looking to the reactions of others for approval and validation not just of your capabilities, but of your value as a human being. Process, craft, and expression matter, as does engagement and feedback that allows you to gauge the depth and power of your work in the name of progress.

But obsessive focus on either can lead to devastating emotional outcomes. It is a very good idea to develop daily practices that allow you to adopt a lens of gentleness, honesty, self-compassion, awareness, and gratitude. And know that both process and service will play important roles in your ability to feel fully expressed and utterly alive.

SHOW ME THE MONEY.

The work of the Performer, like the work of so many of the Sparketypes, tends to have what most would consider a conventional outlet, and then a universe of nonconventional ones. The interesting thing here is that, while most of the other Sparketypes find the easiest path to a comfortable living when pursued along those more conventional paths, for the vast majority of Performers, it's the opposite.

Unlike other Sparketypes, like Scientists and Essentialists, who are naturally drawn to traditional career paths, the vast majority of Performers who pursue their impulse in the most conventional way, often performing arts, struggle to earn a comfortable, full-time living. That is not to say it's not possible. It is, but the percentage of Performers who are able to do it full-time and earn a consistent, comfortable living tends to pale in the percentage of other Sparketypes who generate a comfortable, secure living through whatever more conventional options are available to them.

That said, all is not lost, because the impulse and skills of the Performer are incredibly valuable, in demand, and often very well compensated when they find an outlet in the exponentially larger array of nonconventional opportunities. Performers in business-development or sales roles can create and enliven an interaction or presentation in a way that leads to exceptional outcomes and substantial compensation. Speakers, facilitators, leaders in hospitality, recreation, and beyond find countless opportunities to bring the impulse to their work in a way that makes them come alive and translates into revenue. This impulse and skill, in fact, is both rare and incredibly differentiating in the world of business.

You may also, like so many, find a deeply meaningful blend of nonconventional outlets, mixed with conventional and even other devotions that allow you to tap the impulse with no expectation of compensation beyond the feeling it gives you. We've seen examples of all of these in the stories above. More on this in the "Spark Your Work" chapter. Your work is to find the sweet spot that gives you what you need.

PREFORMER

THE
SAGE
You, in a nutshell.

SLOGAN.
I awaken insight.

Animating impulse.

For Sages, illumination is your call. You live to share insights, ideas, knowledge, and experiences with others in a way that leaves them in some way better, wiser, and more equipped to experience life differently—and maybe sparks something in them that makes them want to learn more.

While there is definitely a process-fulfilled side to the work that makes you come alive, you tend more often to find your fullest expression and get your greatest reward when focused on the impact you have on those you seek to help illuminate and elevate. It's rarely enough to just know your topic well or have command over your craft. You can't just stand in front of a room, or write a book, give a talk, or produce a podcast and feel like you've done what you came to do. Sages want to know what you share actually lands in a way that is understood, integrated, and embodied. When you see the lights of discovery go on in the faces of others, it's magic. But for you, it's not enough to simply convey information; you want those you teach to truly "get it." Comprehension, integration, and understanding is the ultimate goal and the thing that allows you to complete the cycle of illumination.

When you are working in a way that allows you to spend the greatest amount of time immersed in the process of teaching and sharing wisdom, you feel most alive. When the body of knowledge you are teaching and the people you seek to impact are a reflection of topics and communities, visions, interests, ideas, values, and process that you feel intrinsically called to, you become Sparked. When you have control over the process, tools, resources, and vision, you light up. And, most important, when you see the lights of understanding go on in the minds of those you teach, you come alive.

The Sage is also one of the Sparketypes that tends to show up in a central way not just in professional life, but in all aspects of life with friends, family, and pretty much anyone and everyone else. The impulse to illuminate simply cannot be contained.

SAGE

Elaine.

Elaine Montilla (Sage/Maven) is a Sage, and has always been one, in every domain of her life. In fact, for years, her family has playfully called her a preacher, because any time she learns something, she immediately turns around and tells anyone who'll listen what she's discovered. Her friends often ask which degree or certification she's finishing because they know Elaine has an insatiable hunger for knowledge. For her, though, it's not just about knowing. Her Maven impulse to devour wisdom is largely in service of what she'll do with what she learns. Had her Primary Sparketype been the Maker, she'd likely tap her growing body of knowledge to create at a higher level. A Scientist primary would harness the knowledge to more effectively figure out solutions to puzzles and problems.

For years, Elaine could never truly understand why she loved reading and learning so much and, also, why it never seemed to be enough. With the discovery of her Sage/Maven pairing, it all made sense. She learns to illuminate.

In her personal life, she'd gather girlfriends for a "Supersoul" conversation. "It is always a joke," she shared, "because I love listening to their struggles and using the knowledge I have to share insights with them and help them see that life is way more beautiful than their minds want them to believe." That same Sage impulse to teach, illuminate, and elevate has led her to public speaking and advocating for women and minorities in the tech sector. As a senior executive and primary technology leader at The Graduate Center, City University of New York, Elaine regularly shares insights, ideas, and possibilities with her team of IT managers. Building on her focus on diversity in tech and beyond, she founded 5Xminority, an organization on a mission to make workspaces more inclusive, through leadership, educating, and mentoring.

"I come alive," Elaine offered, "when I am onstage or when I answer questions that I know would help other Latinas succeed in tech, like me, and I know that the Sage in me is guiding me."

Learning, to share.

Elaine's story touches on another commonality among Sages. Before you can share, you have to have something worth sharing. This leads many Sages to embrace a path of fierce learning. And, when they learn, it often takes on a different tone. When you're a Sage, your entire way of taking in the world is different, though you may not realize it. Because, for you, learning isn't just a curiosity, it's not just about fascination (though that may be a part of it, especially if your Shadow Sparketype is the Maven). There's almost always something bigger going on.

Dan.

Once a month, for more than a decade, I've been meeting Dan Lerner (Sage/Advisor) for breakfast. Just two old friends, doing lox, bagels, and eggs, black coffee, jasmine tea, and a few extra slices of tomato just in case. Our orders never change.

Over that time, I've learned that Dan devours information, but in a way that is different from me—and, honestly, different from most people I know who are not also wired to share. He pursues knowledge, in no small part, with the intent to integrate disparate bits, then share them as coherent insights as a professor, speaker, and consultant, but also as a father, partner, and friend. That makes him ask different questions, see facts through a different lens, and inquire into nearly every assumption.

After a decade as a classical music agent, then years pursuing the field of excellence and expertise and performance coaching, Dan found himself attending the University of Pennsylvania, where he pursued a master's in applied positive psychology (MAPP). He didn't just attend the MAPP program, he devoured it, engaging the professors during class, and seeking them out in between classes. He wanted to know every aspect of their insights, their research, their applications and questions. He wasn't afraid to challenge, but not in a prosecutorial way, more of an authentic search for the truth. He was asking not just his own questions, but also those of the students he did not yet know he'd be teaching, and to whom he wanted to be able to provide answers.

It wouldn't take long for Dan's wisdom to find an outlet and his Sage impulse to take center stage. Upon graduating, he was invited to become a teaching assistant. The Sage embers began to glow. A few years in, he and a colleague began teaching a new class at New York University on the science of happiness. Stepping into the classroom that first day, Dan knew he'd have to both share and defend his insights before a room of some of the brightest students in the world. Within minutes it became clear he was utterly in his element. He came alive in a way that eluded him when the focus was entirely on learning or coaching. That class, not surprisingly, quickly became the biggest undergrad elective at NYU, with more than six hundred people per semester and a perpetual waitlist.

For most Sages like Dan, it's not enough to cover the basics. Their Sage impulse fuels a quest not just for information, but for depth and nuance on a level that supports their inevitable desire to turn around and say, "Here's what I know; hope it helps."

Just enough to be dangerous.

Interestingly, the impulse to share can sometimes be so strong, it may drive rising Sages to take the teaching reins before they're quite ready. When you're young and the stakes are low, this can be a sweet, fun way of experimenting with the impulse. As you move further into work and life and the stakes rise, things can get complicated, even dangerous.

Christy.

Christy Witt Hoffman (Sage/Essentialist), now a highly sought-after consultant and business strategist, used to come home from kindergarten every day, find her little sister, then teach her everything she learned. By the time her sister went to school, she presented as a little savant. She'd been attending the Christy Academy for two years already. Nobody asked Christy to do this; it was simply the thing she couldn't *not* do. For as long as she can remember, the minute she knew something, she'd turn around and teach it. That same impulse, however, would occasionally trip her up, in the early days of her career in consulting. "Before you can internalize it . . . ," she shared, "maybe even before you know that you have the information, you want to share the information, but you don't know what that information is going to bring, or what information needs to go with that information to make it valuable."

This can lead to the classic blast-and-retreat scenario, where you excitedly eject everything you've learned in a meeting or a classroom or conversation, then the questions come, and you don't have answers. When the stakes are low, it doesn't matter all that much. In fact, that very experience can be a humbling yet hugely valuable opportunity for growth. As the stakes rise, though, so does the potential for harm.

For Christy, instead of feeling dejected or questioning her impulse to share, she realized the fix was to ramp her knowledge discovery and mastery process to a level that matched her impulse to illuminate. Like Dan, a big part of that awakening was learning to ask different questions. Once the "having something to share" engine matched her impulse to share, she became unstoppable, rapidly rising up pretty much any ladder she chose to climb and eventually launching her own organization and consulting business, where she gets to choose what to teach, whose lights to turn on, and how.

Sages who do the work to sync the pace and depth of learning with their impulse to illuminate often find themselves highly sought after, because when they share, everyone knows it'll be worth the listen. They gain the capacity to effectively walk around turning on human light switches all day, while those around them are half grateful, and half wondering what just happened.

A Sage by any other name is still a Sage.

Being a Sage, by the way, does not necessarily mean you call yourself a Sage or even a teacher, or work in a field where it is a clearly articulated part of your job description. Sages exist and, in a supportive and open environment, can thrive and be incredibly valued in nearly any setting, from parenting to teaching to corporate innovation, leadership, administration, speaking, writing, acting, producing, and beyond. You can do the work of the Sage on a one-to-one basis or one-to-thousands, in person or remotely. You can use the vehicle of your voice, body, and presence in a room, a pen and paper, keyboard, video, audio, or really any available mechanism or channel. No matter the mode of engagement or expression, for the Sage it's about the ability to convey ideas, tools, wisdom, and information in a matter that helps others. It's about turning the lights on. Illumination.

Sheila.

Landing the leading role in her middle school play was an epiphany for twelve-year-old Sheila Devi (Sage/Performer). "Performing," she thought. "This will be my life." For years, it was. She turned Harvard down to study theater at Ithaca College, where she deepened into the craft, then pursued an acting career upon graduating. But something in her yearned for more. Sheila eventually moved to Chicago, acting a bit on the side while navigating various jobs. At one point, she even did a stint in the world of culinary arts, cooking and catering. She landed a position in hospitality, was very successful, and rose up the ranks—but again, just wasn't getting what she needed. Her impulse to illuminate remained largely stifled. Around that same time, Sheila stumbled upon the world of coaching. "I want to help people learn to be kind to themselves," she thought. This sounds great. Through the lens of the Sparketype, she reflected, "What I meant was, 'I want to teach people how to be kind to themselves!'"

She quickly excelled, finding her groove as an executive life coach, working with professionals who are "rocking their careers, but at the end of their bandwidth." It was like a nonstop torrent of opportunities to illuminate and elevate.

You might think, "Coaching, right. Shouldn't that be the Advisor Sparketype?" For some, it is. But, as we've seen, nearly any Sparketype can find a way to take the lead in nearly any role, career, or industry. For Sheila, coaching became a vehicle to share skills, practices, and frameworks, and to offer observations and insights in an intimate way.

When we think of the process of illumination, we often picture a person or group of people sharing what they know with others. That, however, is not the only path. The process of sharing and transferring insight can take many different forms, from person-to-person instruction to the creation of experiences, media, or even physical objects that serve the greater purpose of illumination.

Sky.

Sky Banyes's (Sage/Advisor) impulse showed up in a very different way. Sky works as a postdoctoral scientist in the field of physics. Given her background, credentials, and work, you'd think her impulse would find a conventional outlet in the field of education. In ways, it does. But it's also found an unexpected, yet remarkably rewarding outlet in a domain she never expected or saw coming. Years into her career, Sky found herself struggling and, at the cajoling of her therapist, turned to art as a way to process her emotions. She began drawing her internal dialogue and emotions, then started sharing her illustrations on social media. People loved them. Encouraged, Sky spent more time making art. "My illustrations," Sky offered, "have been a means to not only creatively translate my findings from ethereal to tangible, but to share them in the hope of shared genuine understanding." For someone who lives and breathes the scientific method, often ensconced in heavily academic settings, illustration has become a powerful way for Sky to channel her Sage impulse and speak directly to the experiences, hearts, minds, and emotions of a fast-growing global audience who gleefully raise their collective hands to receive her near-daily offerings in the digital realm (@skybanyes).

SAGE

WHAT TRIPS YOU UP.

Sages, like all Sparketypes, are subject to certain fairly common challenges, struggles, and triggers. When faced with these circumstances, you can find yourself spiraling into a dark place, or unable to express yourself on a level that allows you to come most fully alive. Understanding potential stumbling points in advance can help you keep an eye out, and better navigate around them should they come up. If you find yourself in the line of one of these triggering experiences, it's important to know you're not alone and, with patience and intention, you can find a way back to a more alive, expressed place. Here are a few of the common experiences to look out for.

Lack of control.

Sages can sometimes feel stifled by the need to work within systems that constrain their ability to illuminate in a way they know they're capable of, and believe would be of most service. We see this often in public education or institutions and organizations where sharing knowledge is critical, even central to the mission, yet a discrete pecking order limits power and control until you've been in the system long enough to have effectively abandoned hope of transformation. Schools, hospitals, foundations, corporations all risk slipping into this locked-down paradigm. Not infrequently, there is a long-entrenched bureaucracy that impedes innovation, change, and progress and very little individual control or ability to effect change for years, if ever.

Truth is, nobody is happy about this, from the executives and administrators on down to those with essential responsibility to inform and uplift. Sages, who live and breathe illumination, can find this a brutally hard dynamic to survive, let alone flourish in. This is especially true for Sages who share strongly service-driven Shadow Sparketypes, like the Nurturer or Advocate. Because of this, many Sages find themselves grappling with a tough choice. Stay the course and hope that, by the time you've accumulated control and power, you'll still have the fortitude to fight the fight and the organization will have grown more amenable to change. Or create your own channels and mechanisms that exist outside the confines of traditional organizations, where you define the rules of engagement. Many take the latter approach and end up serving the very same community, but with more freedom than an inside-out approach might allow.

Bernadette.

As a young child, Bernadette Johnson (Sage/Maven) was the kid all the other kids turned to when they were in search of answers. She was obsessed with learning, but in her early days, her more introverted nature kept her from taking her seat as a Sage in a more public way. Moving through high school and then college, she began tutoring fellow students, while completing her degree in business.

After graduating, Bernadette headed into the corporate world, spending nearly fifteen years in talent development and performance, eventually rising into senior leadership positions. She was incredibly accomplished, had amassed a certain amount of power, even becoming a central player in developing the organization's culture. Increasingly, however, she yearned for a higher level of control over both the nature of the work and stakeholders she worked with, and the way she embraced the process of illumination.

Shifting to a new organization gave her the ability to facilitate in a way that was more aligned with who she was and what she sought to teach. At the same time, she began to build her own consulting organization, Inspired Action Motivates, allowing her to be highly selective and focus on the specific leadership facilitation that put her Sage impulse in overdrive. She could create the dynamic that she knew both served others best and allowed her to come more fully alive.

For Sages who feel stifled by a lack of control, or even an institution or set of values, rules, or constraints that do now allow you to do what you're here to do, consider the following:

- Consider what you *do* have the freedom, resources, and control to try, in the name of unlocking a higher level of illumination and getting more of what you need.

- Work, over time, to move into a place where you've demonstrated the skill and earned the trust needed to try new things and request resources to implement changes that will lead to a more effective transfer and embodiment of insight.
- Explore the possibility of a "skunkworks" project where you ask for a small amount of time and resources to test new ideas.
- If none of the above help, consider either moving to an opportunity that allows you to more fully express your Sage *or* envision and create your own alternative.

———

Depletion.

Because Sages tend to be more externally service-focused, they can find themselves "over-giving" and becoming physically, psychologically, and emotionally depleted. The risk rises when the system you work within is demanding or all-consuming. It also requires you to devote great amounts of time to both the process of teaching and managing many outside factors, which tend to compound the experience of depletion.

You may be able to sustain this pattern for a while, but it always comes back to haunt you. When your vitality and connection buckets run dry, they will not only grind your happiness and well-being to a halt, they'll also stop you from working on a level that lets you fully express your Sparketype and your potential. This is a common pattern with many Sages who work in fields and environments that are underresourced.

In 2001, I founded a yoga center in New York City. Along the way, working with a team that was way more capable than I, we built a teacher training institute and certified hundreds of teachers from around the world. With time, we started seeing a pattern emerge.

Once teachers began to teach, they started to lose their personal practices. The busier their schedule grew, the less they'd embrace the things that gave them the insight, energy, well-being, equanimity, and experience to be effective teachers. They were all outflow and no inflow. And they'd often end up depleted to a level where they could no longer effectively teach.

In order to counter this, we started sharing this phenomenon in our training programs to increase awareness, then instituted what we called a minimum daily practice requirement, or MDP, comprised of a blend of asana (postures and movement), meditation, and breath work that would take no longer than fifteen minutes.

If you are a Sage, be aware of this potential drain on your ability to give. Commit to filling your tank along the way, if not in the name of taking care of yourself, then in the name of being as effective as possible in your ability to illuminate. If you've done all you can to optimize your well-being and the circumstances under which you teach and still are left empty, you may want to explore a different approach to expressing your Sage call.

SAGE

The self-worth spiral of doom.

While, for some Sages, the impulse to share races past the depth of their sharable wisdom, for others, the opposite becomes a major stumbling point. The feeling of never quite knowing enough, never being good enough at the art and skill of illumination, or holding yourself to the standard of absolute mastery or perfection can stop you from acting on your primary yearning to teach and share. If you find yourself repeatedly uttering some variation of "I don't know enough, I'm not ready, it won't be perfect, I might do harm," you may well have fallen into the Sage's self-worth spiral of doom.

Here's the thing. If your standard for knowing enough and being good enough to teach is absolute wisdom and absolute mastery about every aspect of the thing you want to share, you will never reach that impossible standard.

In certain domains, especially when the stakes are extremely high, it does make sense to know as much as humanly possible before turning around and sharing what you know. If you're training neurosurgeons, you better be a master in the field. The stakes are life and death. But, the reality is, even in the most high-stakes areas, like medicine, international relations, and finance, there is no end to the universe of wisdom or skill. In fact, it's a safe bet that ten years from now, much of what even the smartest, most accomplished Sage knows to be true will be proven false or become dated. At some point, it's important to figure out what your most accessible first step in is, then take it.

Be conscientious, but also let go of unreasonable and irrational prerequisites and just start doing the very thing that most terrifies you. Great teachers teach. They aren't born, they are forged. You cannot be an effective Sage when you do not allow yourself the space and grace to accommodate your own process of growth. This is the foundation upon which so many Sages set about turning on the lights for others. But when it comes to them, it can sometimes be a less forgiving experience.

As Sages, you're charged with knowing the distinction between what researcher Carol Dweck describes as a fixed mindset and a growth mindset and, often, helping to cultivate the latter in those you teach. Those same insights apply not just to students, but to teachers, too. Great teachers don't get great because they've studied how to be great. They get great because they teach, and use their teaching as their own living laboratory to learn and improve. It's the very practice of teaching that most readily reveals not just your blind spots, but also your greatest opportunities for learning and growth. If you want to feel like you're ready to teach, then teach.

SHOW ME THE MONEY.

Expressed in certain ways and settings, your Sage Sparketype may be highly valued and compensated. It is also important to note that many Sages don't actually want to animate their impulse in a traditional setting that revolves around conventional teaching, nor should they feel any sensitivity around the desire to seek other outlets that feel well aligned and may also provide a path to better compensation. The skills and abilities of the Sage—the desire and capacity to illuminate, to turn the lights of awareness, understanding, and insight on—are forever in need in a vast array of industries, organizations, and fields.

Salespeople who are great at illuminating features, benefits, points of differentiation, and reasons why the thing they're offering is exactly what is needed tend to generate high levels of sales, be well compensated, and are also appreciated by customers and clients who get their problems solved and often leave with deeper insights.

Sages in positions of leadership and management often tap their impulse not just to inspire and motivate, but also transfer insight, information, and turn the light of understanding on, cultivating knowledge, autonomy, and competence, along with a greater capacity to deliver outcomes more independently. This often leads to a bump in performance, engagement, and retention that is reflected in opportunity, demand, and compensation.

SAGE

Mental health and healthcare professionals driven by a Sage Primary impulse often leave patients and clients in a better position to understand not just the nature of their challenges, but also the tools, techniques, and practices that can help, along with a clear understanding of how and when to avail themselves of each. A physician once shared that she does not consider an appointment with a patient successful unless that patient can recite back the essence of the conversation and the protocol needed to return to wellness. This approach may well lead to better clinical outcomes, as well as more informed, confident clients and patients and a reputation that generates strong demand for services.

Sage consultants not only guide clients through a process of growth and accomplishment, they also work to ensure their clients know the underlying bases for recommendations and action steps, so they become more self-reliant, capable of making decisions, and able to flourish independently after the engagement wraps. This leads to high levels of success and demand, often accompanied by higher levels of compensation.

Sage-fueled deli-counter workers who share samples and describe how each offering is different with passion and clarity, noting the details, pedigree, what each selection is best for, and how they might land on a customer's palate, not only share fun and insightful facts that make customers feel engaged and informed, but also likely end up selling a lot more product and giving their patrons reasons to come back.

Parents who lead with a Sage's impulse to share what they know give their kids the gift of wisdom, and the building blocks of understanding, self-confidence, and action-taking. The rewards, though not monetary, come in a thousand other ways. Seeing your kids flourish on a whole different level, watching them become more knowledgeable and independent is, as they say, priceless.

And, of course, many Sages often find more direct, conventional outlets, from facilitation and training to speaking, tutoring, and teaching in traditional academic settings. In each of these areas, the impulse, expressed with skill, expertise, and passion can become the source of exceptional compensation. That said, it's also important to acknowledge that many Sages are both called to and find the greatest need in what is often the least (and least fairly) compensated expression of the impulse — traditional teaching settings. The unfortunate truth is that schools are among the places that value Sages the most, but compensate them the least.

If you are called to those settings or students, especially in service of underserved communities, that is a wonderful thing. So many Sages are. Unfortunately, a fairly common part of that bargain is a trade-off in income and control in the name of being able to most directly serve those you're called to help. The promise of summers off, tenure, and pension used to help, but increasingly all three have been vanishing, which is one reason so many Sages have begun to seek employment in other domains where, even if not central to the job, the work and output of the impulse is rewarded at a far more livable level.

Over the last decade, technology, apps, and online platforms like TeachersPayTeachers.com now make it easy for teachers to distill knowledge into everything from video, audio, and other teaching aids to lesson plans that can be purchased by colleagues and used in their classrooms. Other teachers have found ways to access virtual classrooms and video-course platforms to share what they know at scale, making their expertise more available and accessible, while allowing them to craft more sustainable livings.

The big message is that while the traditional classroom teacher model for service and compensation is still alive, there

SAGE

is an ever-expanding universe of opportunities to tap the Sage impulse in different domains and creative ways to craft a level of compensation that lets you both come alive and earn what you need if you're willing to get creative and potentially look outside traditional constraints.

SAGE

THE
WARRIOR
You, in a nutshell.

SLOGAN.
I gather and lead people.

Animating impulse.

There is, and has always been, something inside Warriors that yearns to gather people, organize them, harness their collective energy, assume responsibility, make decisions, and lead them on some form of meaningful, fun, or challenging (sometimes all three) quest, experience, mission, or adventure. For you, it's not just a skill, position, or title as a leader or community organizer, it is a DNA-deep impulse. It is the work you're here to do, even when it's personal, social, and fun.

You might express this through a deeper connection to a specific industry, field, group, or community. It might find an outlet at home, with friends or family. Some Warriors become attached to a particular area of focus, mission, or pursuit for long windows of time. Maybe you captain a team to win a race, game, or season, or summit a peak. Maybe you lead a faculty of teachers to raise graduation rates, or a team to invent and launch a new product, service, or company.

It's also not unusual for your focus or quest to shift over time, especially once you've led others to what you perceive is the pinnacle of where you're all capable of going in that specific context. At that point, you are still wired to gather and lead, but it's time to redirect your energies to a new point A and a new set of quests as you lead people to point B and beyond. Soccer season may be over; you've captained the team that won the championship. That doesn't mean your Warrior goes into hibernation. It means it shifts domains and finds new paths to express itself.

Warriors tend to show their impulse early in life. They're the ones gathering siblings or besties together to plan a cool adventure, celebration, or secret mission—even if they're the youngest. You can find them rounding up friends on the playground, forming teams, leading the charge, and, not infrequently (or always successfully), telling people where to go, what to do, and how. If you're a Warrior, there's a decent chance you were called some version of "bossy" early in life, though at the same time, there'd have been a lot less adventure, fun, and action-taking in everyone's life if you weren't around.

While the Warrior's impulse to gather and lead has a certain process element to it—there are methodologies, skills, and practices that can be mastered along the way—the stronger call and source of fulfillment tends to lie on the service side of the pursuit. When the quest you are leading people toward is a true reflection of your vision, your unique ideas, lens, values, and skills, and you have control over the process, resources, and vision, you become Sparked.

It's important to note, Warriors can also feel highly Sparked even if the goal, quest, or outcome they work to bring people toward never materializes. Joining with others and working toward a specific endpoint is motivating. Even if you fall short of the stated goal, the opportunity to bring people together, rally them toward the cause, then lead them in its pursuit is where so much of the sense of purpose, meaning, expression, performance, and flow comes from.

Being a Warrior often requires a certain benevolent, constructive, and conscious ferocity. Not in a violent way. Not in a fearless way. Not in a heartless, controlling, or domineering way. Warriors can be fiercely fair. They can be fiercely curious. Fiercely convicted or agile. Fiercely collaborative. Fiercely vulnerable and open. Or, fiercely loving. Warriors are not wishy-washy. A certain fierce devotion to people and path must be present in order to do the deeply rewarding, yet sometimes difficult, work of gathering and leading. That ferocity is, in fact, where the moniker *Warrior* comes from. It's not about dominance, force, or pecking order, but rather a willingness to stand in a place of enduring conviction and support, even when things get hard—which, when the stakes rise, they often do.

Linda.

Ever since she was a kid, even though she was the youngest in her family, Linda Blair (Warrior/Advisor) has always been the one who gathered everyone together for meetups and family vacations. In school, she was an athlete, often captaining teams. Figuring out how to bring people together, rally them to be at their best, and work toward a common goal gave her energy. It made her come alive. Same with friends. She's always the one who loves to organize trips, or weekend adventures and outings. Even if someone else takes the lead, she's always asked if she could help.

In the first act of her career, Linda worked as a nurse, primarily with cancer patients. She approached every patient's care as a team effort, where the stakes were often life-and-death. Her Warrior impulse took center stage, bringing people together, coordinating and ensuring every member of the care team, from doctors and nurses to social workers and family, were on the same page and working toward a harmonized goal. Her Advisor Shadow aided the effort, working with each person to share insights, answer questions, and give them what they needed to be active participants in the patient's care.

Expanding on her experience in healthcare and deep desire to be of service to people in a larger context, Linda eventually transitioned out of nursing and into consulting. From the outside looking in, that may seem like a very different direction, but from the inside looking out, her Warrior was simply finding a new channel of expression that was deeply meaningful to her.

In her early days at Deloitte Canada, Linda led a large-scale health industry transformation initiative designed to make information more rapidly available to providers, creating a bit of a bridge experience. She was leading her new team at Deloitte, while simultaneously doing work that improved patient care, yet on a mass scale. Once again, she brought together a disparate team of people to make something extraordinary happen. She tapped her Advisor Shadow to mentor individuals along the way in service of not only helping them flourish, but also equipping everyone to accomplish the bigger vision.

Rising into the role of Chief Experience Officer and becoming a member of the executive leadership team at Deloitte Canada, part of her work involves not just collaborating with her immediate team members, but also translating the visions, ethos, and steps throughout the organization to create a leadership ripple effect that inspires all to join in the quest. It is the perfect integration of her Sparketype and, with thousands of people now in the mix, it's a position that challenges her Warrior impulse in the best of ways, while allowing endless opportunities for it to be expressed.

For Warriors, it's often personal.

While the Warrior impulse to gather and lead can find any number of outlets, it often shows up in areas of interest, devotion, or affiliation that are deeply personal. Many Warriors start as members of a group or community facing a particular challenge. They end up going on their own Heroine's or Hero's Journey, as so many people do. For the Warrior, though, the journey's just begun. It's not enough to have gone on their own adventure and found their way through. They're fueled to bring others together—all those experiencing similar challenges or yearnings—and lead them on a similar journey of discovery, adventure, and awakening. In fact, the joy of scratching their own itch often pales in comparison to the feeling of taking others along a similar journey.

Lisa.

Lisa Wade (Warrior/Maker) has worked in finance for most of her career, with a focus on impact investing. She's driven to work with markets and money in a way that makes a genuine difference in people's lives and in the world. Rising into leadership roles in the industry has given her the opportunity to bring people along with her vision. But it was her experience navigating the overlap between the culture and business of finance and another deeply personal area of her life that led to a powerful awakening around the role of her Warrior Sparketype.

Lisa has been an LGBTQIA+ advocate and community member, but never really saw herself as a Warrior or leader. Upon discovering her Sparketype, something unlocked. "I did a real

WARRIOR

reconciliation of my life," she shared, "and saw that where I was really humming was in my LGBTQIA+ work, where I had stood up to be a leader at my bank and was running the network, inspiring, leading." She began to explore why that experience meant so much to her, realizing she wanted to invest her energy in ways that were completely in service to younger generations, so that they might have a smoother path, more tools and insights and understanding and resources in their finance careers.

Everything she was doing was in the name of organizing and gathering those who might experience a sense of othering in her industry, helping build trust, then working together to navigate to find a place of greater ease. It started with her personal journey, but expanded quickly out to others in the LGBTQIA+ community within the world of finance. That awakening, along with the discovery of her Sparketype, led her to seek to create similar experiences in other parts of life. "It's quite magical when I get it right," she offered. "I am the Warrior/Maker, building great things like partnerships for LGBTQIA+ in my bank, LGBTQIA+ mentoring programs. *And* in impact investing." Full expression, full integration, fully Sparked. And it all started with her own experience and awakening.

Dimple.

Roots in the Clouds founder Dimple Dhabali (Warrior/Advisor) shared a similar awakening, albeit in a radically different context. She's on a mission to "put the 'human' back into humanitarian work." Working in a federal agency with refugees and asylum seekers, her first assignment found her in East Africa interviewing refugees for resettlement. Over the years, that trip would expand into many more as she helped develop policy, and interviewed asylum seekers in the U.S. and refugees from many different countries.

The job was intense, and profoundly gratifying, but it was also psychologically traumatizing. One particular experience in Zambia, interviewing Congolese applicants, survivors of the 1994 Rwandan genocide, and protracted Burundians (individuals who had been born in refugee camps and subsequently had their camps attacked) brought home the brutality of war. She started to experience vicarious trauma, having nightmares, reliving the horrific circumstances in her head. As she researched how to process what she was experiencing, she began to realize she wasn't alone.

A large, global community of humanitarian fieldworkers suffered similar trauma, with devastating effect. She felt called to help, so she launched Roots in the Clouds, an initiative designed to bring fieldworkers together, form a community, equip them with the tools to thrive in the face of sustained, often brutally hard and traumatizing work, and lead them to a place of greater resilience and ease. Her personal experience also compelled her to lead a new initiative in her government work, setting up an in-house resilience and mindfulness program. While it's not a requirement that Warriors rise out of the communities they eventually seek to serve from a place of empathy and shared experience, it is a common story. When that happens, the blend of fully expressed impulse and deeply personal connection to the community and cause makes the call that much stronger— and the reward that much more relevant and meaningful.

WARRIOR

Introverts, extroverts, all are welcome.

If this all sounds very "front and center," you may be wondering, are all Warriors just raging extroverts? Many are, reveling in the public-facing nature of organizing and leading. Many others are not. One of the great Warrior (and Advocate) myths is the tale of the loud, out-front, sword-in-the-air, will-of-steel, cult-of-personality-driven individual who boldly navigates all manner of demons and pitfalls, then takes others along for the ride.

Stories of folks who are wired this way tend to dominate the Warrior legendscape, from movies and books to daily news and social feeds. These tales are fun to tell; they draw people in with colorful personalities, conflict, action, emotion, risk, and adventure. They're also based on an unfortunate cultural misconception — the notion that being out-front, extroverted, and leading from ahead is the only way to gather and to lead.

This is not only wrong, it's harmful. Quieter, more introverted Warriors who not only have no need to be front and center, but would actively rather not be, feel the very same call to bring people together, to build consensus, and to lead them from a more locked-arm, conversational place. Setting the expectation that Warriors must express this impulse in a forward-facing, extroverted way represses and stifles introverted Warriors. It stops them from bringing their incredible energy, effort, insights, and gifts to the people, groups, communities, and organizations they would gladly have served, but for the fact they didn't want to do it the way the culture expects them to. Then, it layers shame on top of the weight of repression for having chosen inaction or quiet action over culturally appropriate, yet personally gutting, expectation.

A few years back, I had the opportunity to spend time in conversation with Sir Richard Branson's mother, Eve. Closing in on her ninetieth birthday, she was alive with stories, ideas, energy, and plans. She wanted to be one of the first passengers to explore outer space in one of Richard's Virgin Galactic vessels. It was clear from whom Richard inherited his sense of adventure.

WARRIOR

Over the last forty years, he has become one of the world's best-known faces in business, innovation, risk-taking, and leadership. He's launched over a hundred companies, employing tens of thousands of people around the globe and transforming everything from music and media to travel, healthcare, communications, and beyond. He is, in every sense of the word, an icon and a leader. And he's an introvert.

Eve recounted how, when he was a young child, Richard was so painfully introverted, she one day put him in the car, drove him a few miles from home, and left him to find his way back expecting he'd have to talk to people to get there. In her mind, it wasn't socially acceptable to be shy. You needed to be able to operate around people and know how to make them feel good.

Over the years, Richard has learned to turn on or step into an extroverted mode, but that's never been his internal wiring, as he detailed in a 2016 article by Will Heilpern in *Inc.* magazine. Between learning how to blend the learned skill of situational extroversion with his more innate introverted way of being, he developed a unique style of leadership that has allowed him to become one of the most effective gatherers and leaders of humans and builders of enterprise, adventure, and impact the planet has ever seen.

If you feel the call to bring people together and, in whatever way feels accessible, work to lead them from where they are now to a better, more enjoyable, more powerful, alive, or uplifted place, do not allow anyone else's expectation about the appropriate social positioning needed to make that happen limit your impulse. Do the thing you're here to do, in the way you're here to do it. If anyone tells you that's not right, know that what they're really saying is, "I would do it differently." Fine, let them. You do you. Lead from who you are, not who you think you need to be in order to do it right.

WARRIOR

Service, not dominance.

Pam Slim (Warrior/Advisor) is one of the most genuine, kind, open, honest, fair, wise, and decent humans you could ever know. She's a lifelong gatherer of people and catalyst for collective action. Pam is also the founder of K'é, "a physical space in downtown Mesa, Arizona, that hosts the The Main Street Learning Lab, a community-based leadership development space that supports and strengthens the work of diverse entrepreneurs— especially entrepreneurs of color and their allies." The word *K'é* is a Diné (Navajo) word that translates roughly to "system of kinship," or the feeling of being deeply connected to a community. Pam was led toward this name because it spoke to what she wanted to create, and also reflected the culture of her husband and children and the central role it plays in their family and life.

While Pam has devoted much of her life to advocacy, her true superpower and deeper impulse is to build intentional community, and to guide members toward constructive, equitable outcomes in a grounded, highly collaborative, yet immensely powerful and respect-fueled way. Pam has a very strong sense of her role in relation to any community she helps catalyze, especially when it comes to relative power. Instead of being front and center, her approach to gathering and leading is more focused on creating the space, offering the invitation, then supporting those from within the community as they step into leadership and work toward specific outcomes.

Leadership, in her eyes, is having the courage to say things that need to be said and creating models that are going to be useful, help people, and, critically, not cause harm or perpetuate models of dominance. "It's my job to be increasing your leadership capacity to make you better, stronger, more capable in what it is that you're doing," she shared. "So you trust your own judgment more, so that you have more discernment, and not so that you're blindly following something that I would say." Organizing and leading, in Pam's experiences, is never about positioning yourself as being stronger, better, wiser, or more powerful, it's about helping people to develop their own leadership capacity, supporting them where you can, then getting out of the way.

This is an important insight. Part of the often hyper-masculine, extroverted, and aggressive mythology around leadership comes with a certain expectation around the assumption of superiority and dominance. It alludes to—or outright demands—that you lead from a pedestal, assuming you're better, smarter, more powerful or capable than those you seek to gather and lead. While this may "work" as a short-term mechanism to rally action, it quickly collapses under the weight of disrespect, repression, disenfranchisement, disaffection, and, inevitably, contempt. It's not only ineffective, it is destructive to those who seek to lead, to the community, to the vision, and to the larger third-party culture that might well have benefited from a more evenhanded, humility-meets-dignity, service-driven approach. And, to you, because it stops you from being able to effectively do the thing you're here to do.

Dominance-driven leadership is, in no small part, a dysfunctional manifestation of super-ego-run-rampant. True leadership, Pam offers, is other-centering, not leader-centering. There is, however, a key quality of Warriors that speaks to a necessary strength, yet in a different way.

WARRIOR

***

Vulnerability is a virtue.

I first met retired U.S. Navy Captain and fast-attack nuclear submarine commander David Marquet back in 2012, as a guest on the *Good Life Project*. He recounted a somewhat terrifying story. Marquet had served in the Navy for many years, eventually earning the opportunity to command a submarine. He studied and prepared fiercely to know everything he could about the vessel and crew he'd be leading. He wanted to do the best job possible. At the last minute, he was reassigned and told he'd be taking command of the USS *Santa Fe*, a nuclear submarine that was largely unfamiliar to him, with a crew that had struggled with morale issues and had the highest attrition rate in the entire fleet. He didn't know the ship, nor was he prepared to take charge of a crew that was in such dire condition. Still, this was his charge, so he stepped into the role and took control, or so he thought.

One day as David discussed a technical issue in the sonar room, he literally had to say, "I don't know." David came to realize that the problem wasn't that he was giving bad orders, it was that he was the one giving orders at all. He knew he didn't know the submarine and wanted the crew to speak up, but ordering them to be proactive and take initiative had no effect as long as he kept telling them what to do. It wasn't until David stopped talking that they felt they could speak up.

In that moment, David realized something had to change. Instead of pretending to know everything and giving unquestionable orders, he decided to step into a place of vulnerability. He acknowledged that his crew knew the ship better than he did and was more experienced and capable at running it than he was and gave them the power to share their wisdom and voice their intentions.

That act of vulnerability landed as a moment of profound integrity, and immediately changed the dynamic. It reignited a sense of respect and ownership at every level, and allowed the crew to feel seen and elevated, while also rising to the invitation to add value to a more collaborative leadership experience. Engagement, performance, morale, and retention skyrocketed, leading the *Santa Fe* to deliver extraordinary ratings. The experience also had a tremendous ripple effect, leading many of the *Santa Fe*'s officers to eventually command their own submarines.

Vulnerability, it turns out, is one of the most powerful tools on the Warrior's toolbelt. It's not about surrendering all decision-making, direction-setting, and action-taking to the will of the community. That, as we all know, can be disastrous and ineffective. It simply means owning the limitations of your knowledge and experience and acknowledging the value of and inviting the contributions of others into the process of gathering, deciding, catalyzing, leading, and lifting.

Shadow power.

While every Sparketype pairing shares a special relationship, often with the Shadow Sparketype being in service of doing the work of the Primary better, Warriors frequently rely on their Shadows to inform "how" they choose to lead. A Warrior/Nurturer, for example, sounds like a bit of an odd combination out of the gate. In fact, it is incredibly powerful. For Warrior/Nurturers, the impulse to gather and lead is very often "operationalized" through the Shadow impulse to see, acknowledge, feel, take care of, and uplift others. In fact, Warriors who have the capacity to tap these nurturing capacities often build astonishingly devoted communities, teams, and organizations. Notice, by the way, I didn't say "tap these Nurturing skills." When we talk about the Sparketypes, we're talking about a capacity that may take a lot of work, but fills you up, rather than a skill that can be learned, but empties instead of fills your tank.

WARRIOR

Similarly, a Warrior/Sage might rely on the impulse to illuminate, share insights, and teach as a primary aspect of leadership. Warrior/Scientists may focus on masterfully solving all the complex problems that inevitably drop into the path of leadership to make the journey more easeful for those who join them. Warrior/Essentialists may well lean on their love of creating order from chaos, developing systems and processes as a way to bring people together and lead them to a desired outcome as efficiently and effectively as possible. You get the point. Yes, these relationships exist across all ten Sparketypes and all hundred possible Primary/Shadow pairings. For Warriors, the Shadow's work often informs the mode of leadership.

WHAT TRIPS YOU UP.

Like every Sparketype, Warriors are subject to certain challenges, struggles, and triggers. Understanding these potential stumbling points, knowing how to identify them, and cultivating the ability to see them coming before they're upon you helps you more effectively sidestep them. This insight also equips you to more constructively respond if and when you find yourself in the midst of these moments that tend to be both fraught and also ripe with opportunities for growth. Here are some of the most common "invitations to reconsider more constructive action."

Right-itis.

Confidence is generally a good thing, but for Warriors, it can be a bit of a double-edged sword. Warriors tend to believe they're right. A lot. This can show up constructively as strength and conviction in the face of challenge. It can look like an ability to trust your point of view, believe your assumptions and visions, and lead others through hard things nobody else sees or believes.

When you are right and are willing to hold the vision long enough for the efforts of those you lead to prove its potential, the impact can be transformative. Problem is, that same instinct can easily tip from good intentions to ego preservation, from possibility into delusion. It can show up destructively as an arrogant and dogged attachment to a wrong point of view or belief in potential, even long after the assumptions and vision that launched the endeavor have been disproven.

The difference between these two expressions of decisiveness often comes down to those two Warriorship touchstones, openness and vulnerability. Stay perpetually open to and in search of the truth, allow yourself the grace to be wrong, and accept the invitation to change course. Own decisions and all that comes with them. You and those you sought to lead may not arrive at the place you hoped, but at least you'll land in the place you are with your dignity and their trust intact.

Decision and direction by committee.

Warriors often hate committees, unless they're leading them and have final say. Granted, decision by committee tends to be agony for many people, but for Warriors with a strong sense of identity tied to a specific idea or ideal of what the process and outcome should look like, being hindered or having their vision diluted by the input of others can be frustrating. This is especially true when the stakes of inaction are high, and time spent in conversation and negotiation increases the potential for harm and complications.

WARRIOR

At the same time, effectively organizing and leading anyone to go anywhere worth going is rarely done alone. Not only is it critically important to share the effort of leadership within a team of co-leaders, it's also a great idea to have a set of trusted advisors to turn to outside your colleagues (more on this in a minute).

That doesn't mean Warriors should surrender every important decision to the democratic process or a committee vote. Surrender is not the same as inclusion, integration, and thoughtful consideration. Warriors can still be strong and decisive, and also consider the insight and input of others who've demonstrated the potential value of their contribution. If you're a Warrior, open yourself to the possibility that, while colleagues need to earn your trust, they may also become amazing allies and catalysts, even teachers and mentors, when you create the space for them to participate in the leadership experience and open yourself to the possibility that you just might not know everything.

WARRIOR

Beside, not ahead or above.

Because Warriors are in a position to transform not only the belief systems of those they lead, but also the lives, work, and understanding of possibility, self-worth, and impact of those who might come along, they risk being viewed as being, in some way, "above" those they lead. Some might even enjoy the sense of power, prestige, and opportunity this perception creates, and foster it themselves. Taken to the extreme, this can lead to a bit of a complex. You buy into a false narrative that you're uniquely skilled, gifted, or graced with the ability to do for others what no one else can. You aren't just a leader, but a savior.

This can be problematic on two levels. For the Warrior, it can lead to arrogance, narcissism, and grandiosity. It can cloud your judgment, make you feel invincible, and lead to wrongheaded, inequitable, or harmful decisions that put you and those you lead at risk. It can also lay the groundwork for opportunistic and potentially unfair power dynamics and abuse.

Being proud of accomplishing hard things and celebrating those wins with your colleagues and community is a great thing. Celebrate it. Share in the journey and the accomplishment. But always remember, at the end of the day, Warriors lead as an expression of devotion and service. The impulse is not about placing yourself above or ahead of others, but about seeing and holding a vision, then bringing others—often members of a community to which you also belong—along in pursuit of a common end. Think humility and fellowship, not arrogance and dominance.

When impulse outpaces ability.

Similar to Sages and Advisors, the impulse to gather and lead is often so strong, and so apparent early on, that it outpaces the skill and experience needed to be effective. The effort and skill needed to gather people in the name of a quest often pales in comparison to the wisdom, experience, and skill needed to navigate the complex social, power, and interpersonal dynamics that often arise in the pursuit of a meaningful goal, especially one that takes time to achieve.

Young Warriors may find themselves presented with the opportunity to step into an organizing and leadership role, not because they're ready, but because they're willing (especially when the endeavor's waters are treacherous and no one else wants the job). They may say *yes*, excited to let loose the Warrior impulse that lives within them and show what they're capable

WARRIOR

of. On the one hand, it's often these "in over your head" experiences that lead to growth and prepare you to be a more effective Warrior. On the other, it's important to keep exploring where capability, desire, stakes, risk of harm, and opportunity intersect.

Remember, when you're a Warrior, it's not just you, or your personal growth or reputation, that are on the line, it's every person you seek to serve, gather, and lead. Before saying *yes*, always take a moment to consider what the stakes are, whose stakes they are, and if you're ready for any given opportunity— so that you don't end up saying *yes* to something that is likely to end in calamity.

A lonely path: build your council.

Angie Cole (Warrior/Scientist) has been the person who rounded up friends to go on adventures since she was five years old on the playground. Bringing people together and leading them on quests, crusades, and journeys wasn't so much a conscious thing, it was just who she was. When she first discovered her primary Sparketype was the Warrior, she didn't want it to be. It sounded too bold, too solitary. She was scared of it and resisted it, even though she knew deep down the description fit her to a T. What was going on? Where was the resistance coming from?

"Being a natural leader brings a sense of 'otherness,' separateness, and loneliness," she shared. "It can be tricky to find and keep true peers, specifically Warrior peers who can and are willing to be collaborative." Angie's hunch speaks to a common phenomenon among Warriors. Gathering and leading can be incredibly fulfilling and unifying, yet also incredibly isolating. Leading is hard. Navigating relationships is hard. Managing the emotions, logistics, dreams, desires, hopes and fears, implosions, and moments of expectation that inevitably drop into your path can be hard. Warriors often grapple with high levels of uncertainty and high stakes, constantly shifting circumstances, fragile social, political, and power dynamics and, equally challenging yet far less often acknowledged, their own inner spin.

Some of this is appropriate and healthy to share among colleagues, collaborators, and fellow members of leadership teams, sometimes even within the larger group or community. As we've seen, vulnerability and honesty are powerful traits for Warriors to embody. But, not all of it. And not all the time. Some of the tests and challenges will be about members of the groups and communities they seek to lead, or even their fellow Warriors. There is also a fine line between expressing vulnerability and losing the confidence of those you lead. Because of this, Warriors cannot always turn to those same people for communion, commiseration, guidance, and resolution. Even when you respect and want the best for them.

Rare is the Warrior who is capable of going it alone. It's not impossible, but it can turn a challenging yet rewarding process into a brutally isolating season that helps neither you nor those you seek to lead. Angie knew, for her, the answer was to find a way to gather and lead, but not have to go it alone. Having an outside person or group to turn to—a sort of council of Warriors—can be a source of insight, support, and also serve as a neutral release valve in what sometimes feels like a leadership storm. That is exactly what Angie created, and it was transformative. Take the time to find your people. They may not all be Warriors. Maybe they're Advisors or Nurturers or Sages and Scientists. Each contributes value, but the benefit of being in a community with other Warriors who are leading not with, but alongside, you is that you share a common experience,

WARRIOR

speak a common language, and can see and support each other in a very different way.

SHOW ME THE MONEY.

While many people can learn the skill of gathering and leading and be great at it, for Warriors, the impulse is primal. You've likely been acting on and honing the skill side, without even realizing it, since you were a kid. Warriors in conventional roles and industries are often highly sought after and exceptionally well paid. They are viewed as the ones who make things happen and often sustain their efforts even in the face of hardship. They are in demand because of their skills and clarity of purpose, but also because they gather and lead, not just because it's their job, but because it's a pure expression of who they are and what they do. The very existence of that primal impulse often sustains them where others who are fueled more by obligation and skill fall down or step away.

In business, this can lead to roles in management and leadership. They are easily able to rise up the rungs of the leadership-centric, aspirational ladder so many want to climb, finding new opportunities and higher value and compensation along the way. While this impulse and skill set is deeply valued in nearly every domain, industry, and pursuit, it may not be as well compensated in non-business areas. In the worlds of social ventures, causes, foundations, aid work, or community organizing, strong Warriors will always be in demand, though the work will not always give you what you want or need financially.

When you feel called to express your impulse in one of those domains, you may find yourself looking to create an alternative vehicle to gather and lead that integrates the best of both worlds.

WARRIOR

We see this in the creation of "for purpose" corporations. You may also find yourself exploring a more blended path, where you express some of your Warrior impulse in a field that does compensate you well, but may not be fully aligned, then allocate the balance of your Warrior bandwidth to be of service to a person, community, pursuit, or field where compensation is lower or even not a part of the equation. More on this in the "Spark Your Work" chapter.

The important thing to know is that the work you are compelled, on a DNA level, to do is critically important, highly valued, and, depending on the path you choose, capable of nearly any level of compensation.

WARRIOR

THE
ADVISOR
You, in a Nutshell.

SLOGAN.
I guide to grow.

Animating impulse.

For the Advisor, the work of coaching, mentoring, and advising fills you like nothing else. You're the person who swoops in, develops sustained, personal relationships, most often with individuals or small groups, cultivates trust and confidence, and creates the safety needed to guide people in a hands-on, engaging way toward a desired end. It's all about wisdom, trust, confidence, curiosity, presence, and guidance (though, as you're about to see, not necessarily in the way you think). Whoever you work with, their win is your win.

While you see yourself as someone who is wise and skilled, for you, it's less about illumination or teaching a particular body of knowledge the way a Sage might be drawn to do, and more about the interactive experience of walking people through a process of problem-solving, application, achievement, and, ultimately, growth.

It's also not just about the outcome. The aspiration is not just to get them to the place they yearn to be. More important is the depth of connection, the nature of the relationship between you and your advisees, the joy of the trust that you cultivate, and knowledge that you're making a genuine difference. For many advisors, it is also about helping others develop their own inner trust, competence, confidence, and self-reliance so that, when the time is right, you can step away and watch them soar.

Because of the intensely relational nature of their impulse, Advisors tend to be strongly externally gratified. They need to be interacting with others to truly come alive. While they may be incredibly experienced, wise, and have developed their own mastery of the craft of advising, the deeper, more meaningful satisfaction comes not from process, but from service. It's about the quality of the relationship and the ability to make a real difference. Advisors are nourished knowing they've created the context and container to allow others to go deep, get open, and trust in the integrity and wisdom of the relationship.

When Advisors are working in a way that allows them to spend the greatest amount of time immersed in the process of guiding in a hands-on, relationship-driven way, leveraging their insights and experience to a fiercely desired outcome, they feel most alive. When they have control over the process, resources, and approach to growth they believe will yield the best results, they become Sparked. When their work helps a client, mentee, or advisee achieve what they're working toward, Advisors feel deeply satisfied.

ADVISOR

Charlie.

Charlie Gilkey (Advisor/Scientist) deployed for Operation Iraqi Freedom as a transportation platoon leader. He was later promoted to a Battalion Plans Officer and Battle Captain. Upon returning, he planned and executed joint force training exercises that provided real-world combat convoy scenarios in order to prepare soon-to-deploy troops for the environment in which they'd be operating. He is possessed by the quest to figure out solutions to complex problems in a way that is both efficient and effective. In his role in the military, a single mistake didn't risk just time and money, but lives. Beyond mastery of the process of figuring things out, which is the work of his Shadow, Charlie was always acutely aware of and deeply interested in the human side of every task, process, and mission. To this day, he wants to know the *why*, and the impact on the people who'll be touched by both the problem and the universe of potential solutions of anything he's involved in. He's perpetually asking, *How will this help others help themselves?* A huge part of his motivation is to create systems and processes that foster independence and cultivate self-reliance.

Part philosopher king, process-whisperer, professor, and action-catalyst, since moving into the civilian world, Charlie now spends much of his time deploying his impulse to guide and advise in the domain of business, working with senior leaders.

He does all of this deep thought and problem-solving not just in search of an answer, but because he wants to be able to serve his clients at the highest level possible. Over the years, as the founder of Productive Flourishing, a strategic business consultancy, he's worked with everyone from startup founders to executive leadership teams in large organizations, and from educators who are developing next-generation paradigms for higher education to creative professionals who struggle to turn ideas into

ADVISOR

actions and actions into outcomes. That last part has, in effect, become Charlie's calling card.

When Gilkey walks into a room, stuckness walks out.

Along the way, he realized, no matter the industry or level, his clients invariably struggled mightily with the same thing. So he began training his eye for effectiveness and efficiency on his own process, distilling his lens on making things happen into a clear, actionable methodology. After years of testing and refining, Charlie shared this methodology in the book *Start Finishing: How to Go from Idea to Done*. Bringing his Start Finishing methodology to the world has allowed Charlie to effectively scale the impact of his Advisor/Scientist impulse, while working in a hands-on way with a select group of private clients, knowing his ideas will ripple out into the lives of so many others. The book also establishes him in a more public way as the founder of a methodology that, for Advisors, can help open doors to higher levels of demand, compensation, and choice of clientele.

The best Advisors don't.

It's not unusual for those who have the Advisor impulse to say something like, "I'm the one people have come to for as long as I can remember for advice. They've got a problem, I'm the one they want answers from." We tend to associate the role of the Advisor as the deliverer of answers. And there is some truth to that. But the deeper truth is that great Advisors are less often the sources and more often conduits for the emergence of deep insights and solutions.

The more accomplished an Advisor becomes at the craft of advising, the less telling and the more listening they do. They understand and have cultivated the ability to create the context for inquiry, understanding, and awakening. They offer prompts and ask questions designed to elicit critical information, then provide insightful frameworks based on experience and intelligence designed to help those in their trust arrive at the best possible answers, actions, insights, and outcomes. This is the magic that engenders not only extraordinary breakthroughs, but also self-efficacy, self-confidence, and independence, rather than dependence and insecurity.

Michael.

Michael Gervais is a high-performance psychologist who has worked in an advisory role with many of the top-performing athletes and professionals in the world, from Olympians to the Seattle Seahawks to musicians and Fortune 100 CEOs. He is also an author, researcher, speaker, cofounder of Compete to Create (a digital platform focused on mindset training), and host of the *Finding Mastery* podcast. Michael shares, "I don't give advice. I made a pact that I'm not giving advice. I know too much about how complicated it is to arrive at a conversation, and so I feel it's a total disservice/shortcut approach to learning to give advice." He then shared a three-level model he calls the Bands of Coaching developed in the context of physical coaches, but highly relevant in the broader domain of Advisors.

The amateur coach talks a lot, gives a lot of advice, but the accuracy of their advice is often questionable and their approach, to a certain extent, stifles self-awareness and self-discovery. Performance coaches give highly accurate information, along with a bit of advice based on experience, most often as a way of occasionally shortcutting a realization.

Elite coaches are incredibly rare. They don't say much, but instead, ask a lot of questions. "They understand not only the arc of the person, but the arcs of people," Michael offered, "and they're so connected to the insights and the intel and the understandings of the person they're working with that they know they have to observe in a world-class way. And part of that observation is learning through questions." They are masters at nuance, deduction, and have the capacity to elicit insights that land more as self-revelation than information. They are profoundly relational and, in the end, transformational. Not surprisingly, it takes years, maybe decades, of experience and study to bridge the gap from amateur to performance to elite. The journey requires dedicated, purposeful practice and the guidance of increasingly skilled Advisors.

Karen.

Toronto-based executive coach and founder of Parachute Executive Coaching Karen Wright (Advisor/Warrior) has been a trusted guide to leaders in industry for more than two decades, focusing on leadership development, change management, and strategic growth. Working with CEOs and senior leaders, often at times of great disruption and transition, she draws upon decades of experience, but also many years of training across multiple domains. She stepped into this path after having earned an MBA at the Ivey School of Business, then rising up the ladders of some of the largest organizations in the world. Karen knows the professional, social, political, and interpersonal dynamics that define her clients' days intimately. She has lived them, and has spent years deepening her skills of observation and insight. She's a master at her craft, in the league of Michael Gervais's elite coaches.

Karen described the opening minutes of a typical coaching session. She walks into an office, often inhabited by a CEO, sits down, and asks that all technology be shut down or moved away, creating a container that is both safe and sacred. She has no agenda beyond a commitment to being utterly present, deeply generous, and fiercely honest. She owes that to her clients, because she's often the only one who will be. One of the few they trust to be. Nearly every session starts with three simple words: "So, what's up?" Where they go next is guided entirely by how her client responds in the moment. With complete trust, they'll end up where they need to be.

Karen knows, after decades of experience and a devotion to her own mastery and growth, she is most of service when she creates the space for others to share, listens not just to what's being said but also to what's being expressed in a thousand ways beyond language, then joins them in a space of curiosity and generosity. She is there, more than anything, to notice, to reflect, to query, and to trust that the quality of the container, the precision of her questions, and the depth of the relationship will allow whatever insights are needed to emerge. And, without fail, they do. This is the power of an Advisor who truly understands the path and commits to her own pursuit of excellence.

Safety first, or nothing.

If the skills of observation and inquiry are the water and sunshine that allows the Advisor to effectively do what they're here to do, the ability to create a context or container of safety and trust is the soil in which the relationship and the outcomes grow. Without that, nothing happens. There is no openness, no vulnerability, no honesty, and no space for processing, inquiry, integration, revelation, or transformation. For the client, success is no longer on the table.

For the Advisor, it's an impenetrable roadblock to their ability to do the very thing they're here to do. The first step to creating

ADVISOR

this container is awareness of its importance. Then comes an understanding of the elements of safety and trust, things like honesty, presence, vulnerability, and more. This takes time and skill. But it also requires a certain amount of control over the setting, paradigm, and interaction, which can be a big challenge for Advisors who are newer to a culture or work within a paradigm that makes it brutally hard to cultivate.

Avanti.

Avanti Kumar Singh (Advisor/Nurturer) was building a career in emergency medicine in Chicago. She was good at it, but also increasingly distressed by the system, the rules and constraints and approach to helping that defined her professional life and much of her waking hours. Avanti had an intuitive understanding that to truly express her Advisor/Nurturer Sparketype, to help people get better, she needed the time, resources, permission, and ability to go deeper with them. She needed to see them and their lives in a much more complete, nuanced, and honest way and create the freedom to build a trusting relationship and openness that might more readily lead to revelation and healing.

That was brutally hard to do in the context of a fast-paced, time-compressed, quota- and data-driven paradigm of medicine in which she was building her career. She had a decision to make. Avanti's parents had immigrated to the United States from India. From a young age, she'd been exposed to Ayurvedic healing traditions. As her disillusionment with Western medicine rose, she became increasingly interested in Ayurvedic medicine with its focus on relationships, nuance, context, spaciousness, and consideration of the fuller picture. She was drawn to the fundamental tenet that no person heals another, but rather that given the right context, wisdom, and prescription, we all have the ability to create an environment that is optimal for our bodies to return to a state of well-being. Part of that context was a certain reverence for the individual, the relationship, and the quality of the interaction and container. It allowed people to feel seen, heard, and safe. This appealed deeply to her Nurturer Shadow as well, taking care to create safety and ease. From that foundation, her Advisor could step in and engage in a way where true growth could emerge.

Avanti began to study Ayurvedic medicine with the same rigor she studied Western practice. She eventually transitioned out of the Western paradigm that made it hard to practice in a way that not only served her clients on a deeper level, but also allowed her to more fully express her Sparketype. Building on the Ayurvedic approach, she was able to create a far more spacious container of trust, safety, and grace, one that let her truly understand the experience of her patients and settle into a mode of service where she could more effectively guide their healing journey.

The power of exquisite attention.

As Gervais noted, and Avanti demonstrated, creating safety and trust is a critical part of the Advisor's work, as is putting in the years or decades to build a deep well of wisdom and experience needed to understand how to guide others in an informed and accurate way. But maybe the single greatest capability and contributor to powerful outcomes (and Advisors feeling awesome about their work) lies in the skills of observation. Not just any observation, though—we're talking ninja-level noticing. The ability to flip an internal switch and drop into a state of sustained awareness, presence, and attentiveness.

ADVISOR

Awareness is your capacity to notice everything from environment, context, and subtext to the cognitive, emotional, and energetic state of the people with whom you're engaging, even if not a single word is said. It is your ability to see, not just the representations of reality you've become accustomed to, but rather reality itself. Presence is your ability to notice where your mind is at any given time, then redirect it back into the present moment, circumstance, and interaction. It's the wrangling element of attention. Your physical presence is a part of it, but it's much more about your emotional, creative, and cognitive capacity, what Ram Dass called *be here now*. The way your body shows up is simply a reflection of where your mind is at any given moment. Attentiveness is where intention enters the experience. It's about how, when, and where you choose to cast the spell of attention in a way that is experienced as generous, revelatory, and rare.

Together, these components create an effect I've come to know as "exquisite attention." When you and those you seek to guide step into the realm of exquisite attention, something on the level of magic unfolds. There is an immediate sense of ease, an experience of shared knowing, of seeing and being seen and heard, witnessed and held. It is safe and also alive with trust and truth. In this space exists grace. A moment of shared recognition. Without even offering a single word of advice, insight, framework, or plan of action, the very experience of exquisite attention is transformative.

I've seen this in my own work over the years, whether teaching yoga students or interviewing guests in the podcast studio. I remember stepping into the practice room in my yoga studio in the early aughts, leading forty-something students, mat-to-mat in a sweaty, darkened space, flowing, breathing, feeling. Not yet practiced at the art of exquisite attention, on random nights I

ADVISOR

would find myself dropping into it, without understanding why or knowing how to re-create it. When I was in it, that nine-hundred-square-foot room became my world. Nothing outside the walls existed. It was as if I was seeing and feeling every person's energy, every fight, hug, win, loss, commute, cry, hope, desire, and fear. Reading and reacting, calling out sequences in response. Students would walk out of the room and invariably ask some version of "what just happened in there?" I honestly didn't know.

As I've become more aware of the answer to that question and the power to transform a moment that comes from cultivating exquisite attention, I've learned to seed the state in a more on-demand way, always in the name of connection and elevation. In the recording studio, my guests and I often drop into the space of exquisite attention in a matter of minutes. I liken it to an invisible cloak of safety, grace, and generosity of spirit that wraps around us, allowing the conversation to go places neither of us have gone before, or planned to go then. Those same breath-buzzed comments my yoga students would share on the way out of class nearly two decades ago have become a regular part of the post-recording conversation as we step out of the studio and back into the swirl where, all too often, nobody is really paying attention to anything or anyone anymore.

Interestingly, during the pandemic, when we were forced to switch to remote recording, I was concerned that we might lose this critical element. I wondered if it would somehow denigrate the sanctity of the container, forestall the ability to cultivate exquisite attention, and degrade the depth and quality of the conversation. Not just because my guests would be distracted, but because I would. No doubt, that unplanned switch to a virtual format had some effect. Still, I was surprised by how readily the experience of exquisite attention could be re-created in a virtual environment when you understand its importance and do the work to build the skill.

We live in a world that is so dominated by pace and fragmented presence, the simple act of giving another not just your time, but your exquisite attention is experienced as a gift—a rare offering in a sea of distraction and invisibility. On the one hand, this is profoundly sad. On the other, it's a call to action, one that is relevant to every person and every interaction, but is also success-critical to the work of the Advisor. The best Advisors understand the power of this offering and do the work to cultivate the learnable skill of exquisite attention, knowing its effect alone, devoid of answers and advice, is likely more than half the benefit of the advisory relationship. And the deepening of the relationship is a big part of the reward to the Advisor.

Advisors, by any other name, are still Advisors.

It's easy to pigeonhole Advisors into obvious industries, organizations, jobs, titles, or roles, like consultants, coaches, therapists, and teachers. As with every Sparketype, *obvious* does not mean *only*. In fact, the Advisor impulse is expressed in so many different fields and forms, whether or not you associate with any of the above titles. This sometimes leaves the impulse somewhat obscured, especially when it emerges in ways that are nontraditional, from a career standpoint.

Arian.

Arian Moayed (Advisor/Maker) has been performing for his entire adult life, with leading roles as an actor in everything from Emmy Award–winning TV shows to TONY-nominated theater, to major motion pictures. Looking at his career from the outside in, you'd think, "What a performer," and assume his Sparketype is, in fact, the Performer. It must be—that's been his life. Except, it's not. Arian, it turns out, is an Advisor/Maker. Yes, he loves the collaborative, expressive experience of performing, but there's a deeper impulse that fuels him. It's all about guiding, mentoring, and with the support of his Shadow, making. Arian's Advisor impulse shows up when he steps into the role of writer/director, which is becoming an increasing part of his work. But it is most radiantly on display in the work he does through Waterwell, the theater/film production and arts education venture he cofounded.

At Waterwell, he helps guide the growth of New York City teachers and sixth- to twelfth-grade students with free theater training programs. On the surface, it's about performance, but Arian's deeper call is to tap the vehicle of performance to explore citizenship, service, equality, advocacy, and justice. It's a channel to help guide students along a process of discovery and growth, as they learn what it means to be good and to be human in the world. "Reading my Sparketype validated many of my own decisions and made me feel less . . . well . . . crazy," Arian shared, "Often I bring in young artists just making their own way into our Waterwell offices and I get asked, 'Why are you helping me?' And the response is that I'm interested in helping young folks make their own way."

Arian has also become increasingly involved in mentoring and advocating on behalf of immigrant communities, an experience to which he is deeply connected. His family immigrated to the U.S. from Iran when he was a young child, landing in Chicago, where he developed an intimate understanding of what it feels like to be othered. For Arian, whether he calls himself an advisor, coach, mentor, teacher, or friend is irrelevant. It's all about the opportunity to build meaningful relationships with people to whom he feels a genuine connection, then help guide them along a process of discovery, agency, and growth.

Even Advisors need Advisors.

Whether you're working toward an individual goal, or as a team, group, or even organization, it is nearly impossible to achieve anything extraordinary without access to a skilled Advisor. That, by the way, applies to Advisors as well. To become world-class at your craft, you need help.

K. Anders.

Cognitive psychologist and researcher K. Anders Ericsson spent much of his adult life researching the field of excellence and expertise, possessed by a question, What do those who achieve at the highest level do differently? He deconstructed the practices, habits, and work of elite performers across a wide array of fields and began to notice a shared phenomenon he called *deliberate practice*, which is an approach to practice where every action is focused around a goal that is narrow, measurable, specific, and growth-oriented. Every iteration is examined, then adjustments are made toward improvement.

To reach a place of excellence or expertise in any domain takes deliberate practice over thousands of hours and often many years. It is psychologically and emotionally grueling. As Anders shared with me in conversation on the *Good Life Project* podcast, if you're having fun, you're likely not engaging in deliberate practice.

Question is, if deliberate practice is so unpleasant, and you need to embrace it not for weeks or months, but rather for years or even decades in order to reach the upper echelons of excellence and expertise, how does anyone sustain that level of effort? It is, in fact, nearly impossible to succeed at this level without the guidance, insight, compassion, and expertise of someone in your corner who is capable of doing the work of the Advisor. You may call that person an advisor, coach, mentor, teacher, parent (that gets sketchy). Friends or training partners may even fit the bill, if they're skilled and called to deliver in the way an Advisor must.

Ericsson began to focus in on the critical importance of this relationship in his later work and in his book, *PEAK: Secrets from the New Science of Expertise*. He described the evolution of deliberate practice under the guidance of a trusted coach or mentor—someone doing the work of the Advisor—as not just deliberate, but purposeful practice.

There will be times where you hit a wall. Getting through it is not about motivation or inspiration or desire. It is about having access to someone who knows you, sees you, understands why you've come to this stuck point, and can share the insights, frameworks, prompts, and guidance needed to move through this threshold in a way you could not do yourself. When you think about it, this is proven out in the real world.

Professional athletes don't outgrow the need for coaching, but rather grow into deeper, more engaged relationships with coaches who are skilled enough to help at higher and higher levels of performance. It is tough to rise up in the world of business without a trusted advisor helping you navigate the journey. Even at the level of CEO, the best of the best in business have someone, most often outside the organization, with whom they've developed a deep bond of trust and to whom they hold themselves open to honest guidance. And, just like those they advise, Advisors need their own trusted Advisors in order to continue with their own growth.

ADVISOR

Simple truth, if you want to keep growing, no matter the domain, you need help. The best Advisors are also advisees.

WHAT TRIPS YOU UP.

Advisors, like all Sparketypes, tend to become triggered by a fairly common set of circumstances and experiences. When this happens, it can lead to feelings that range from frustration and agitation to anger, fear, anxiety, paralysis, and more. Because the fundamental nature of the Advisor's impulse demands a certain level of intimacy with those you seek to serve, challenges and stumbling points can also feel deeply personal. And, because it's not just you, they can take skill, understanding, and vulnerability to navigate. Here are some of the most common challenges that arise for Advisors, with thoughts on what to be on the lookout for, and how to handle them if they should arise.

When clients seek validation over insight.

Just because someone asks for your help, even pays you for it, doesn't mean they're open to receiving it. When an advisee seeks your help but then doesn't "let you in" or act upon it, Advisors can become incredibly frustrated. At first glance, this may seem like a fictional issue. Who asks for help, pays for it (sometimes very well), then refuses to receive or act on it? What an utter waste of all parties' time, energy, and devotion. Indeed, it is. It happens with stunning frequency, sometimes to devastating psychological effect for Advisors.

Not infrequently, people, groups, or organizations will seek out the help of an Advisor, expressing a desire for guidance toward a particular growth goal. But under the surface, there is a different, often stronger, compulsion. Instead of insight and growth, they're seeking validation of their ideas, plans, strategies, approaches, desires, conclusions—even of themselves as human beings. If, as an Advisor, you happen to guide them in a way that validates their underlying premise, they may well leave satisfied. If, however, the experience speaks to the intelligence of another way, they'll often reject both the insights and you. They may even rail against the experience and wisdom generated, not because it was bad or wrong, but because it didn't give them the cover they were seeking.

This can be an incredibly disconcerting experience for Advisors. Part of your reward as Advisor is derived from the integrity and depth of the relationship, trust, and confidence formed between you and your advisees. Another part lies in the integrity of the insights and opportunity for genuine growth and constructive outcomes. When the quest for validation derails aspects of this, a big part of the nourishment you get from the work is taken away. Your Advisor impulse cannot express itself, and you lose the ability to come alive. It's not about satisfying an ego-driven expectation that every advisee will "do what you say." As noted above, the most skilled Advisors don't often tell you what do to, but rather observe and inquire. It is about an advisee's willingness to explore and consider insights and ideas that may be contrary to the ones they started with, regardless of the final decision they might make, or the path they might choose to take.

Keep your eye out for this dynamic. When first deciding whether to engage with an advisee or not, ask questions about deeper assumptions, expectations, and prior engagements. A series of failed engagements focused around the same area they're inquiring about is a potential red flag that they're shopping for

ADVISOR

validation instead of insight. If you find yourself in the middle of this dynamic with anyone from a client to a friend or family member, remember, sometimes the job of an Advisor is to have hard, honest conversations that confront another's hidden desire not for insight, but rather validation. Advisors need to be willing to "go there," or risk finding themselves potentially well compensated, yet frustrated and empty.

<hr/>

When impulse outpaces ability.

We all start where we are, as beginners. That's not a bad thing. How do we get better? Training, mentoring, study, reflection, integration, and experience. Want to be a better Advisor? Advise. But also, be aware of what you don't yet know, and are not yet capable of doing. Once you begin to move out of the safety of a small circle of friends and family and the complexity and stakes rise, a well-intended, confident, yet under-equipped Advisor can at times do more harm than good. It's important to be aware of the relationship between the desire to serve and the ability to serve, especially when the demands of a person or group or organization's goals and challenges become increasingly complex, and the stakes of failing rise.

Sure, being an effective guide, coach, mentor, or advisor is part intuition, but intuition alone may lead not only to wrong, but also indefensible or even harmful outcomes. Work with your impulse, honor it, build around it, but also own the current edge of your capabilities. It is important for Advisors to seek their own advisors, training, education, and growth. Sometimes this looks like degrees, other times it comes from a long-term coaching or mentoring relationship, certification, licensing, or other experience. Many times, it's a blend of all of the above. The big takeaway: invest in building skill, wisdom, and experience around your intuition, so that you know you can rely on proven, effective, harm-reducing approaches to helping people in the best possible way. As the ancient Greek physician Hippocrates reminds us, "first, do no harm," then do good work.

Savior syndrome.

Developing deep and trusting relationships with advisees can be a meaningful part of your satisfaction. The relationship can also be at risk of becoming too "you-centered." When the ego becomes too big a player in the advising dynamic, your gratification and need to play the role of savior or be in a position of perceived superiority or dominance may become unhealthy both for you and for those you might advise.

In the early days, when Advisors tend to fall into the "telling people what to do" trap more readily, it can be easy to start to feel like your direct instructions are the source of, rather than catalysts for, your clients' decisions and actions, which are always the ultimate source of success. This is especially true if you happen to find yourself in a bit of a winning streak. The ego begins to think, "I am brilliant, I can do no wrong, I am the real reason for all these people's incredible outcomes." Then, if you stay in the game long enough, reality starts to set in. Clients will stumble, sometimes mightily and repeatedly, especially when the stakes are high. Fear and anxiety without true insight and intelligent tools leads to bad decisions. Just when you think you are the universe and can do no wrong, the real universe laughs, and decides it's time for a lesson. If open to it, rising Advisors will see this and, rather than blaming clients or advisees for either ignoring or poorly executing their advice, they'll realize

ADVISOR

their invitations and insights may not have been quite so wise, step back into a place of vulnerability, and be open to the fact that there's a lot of learning left to do. For all of us.

No matter where you are in your advising journey, remember, it's not about you; it's about those you seek to serve. You are not anyone's savior. Your reward is not that your clients' successes become attributed to you, but rather the opportunity to develop deep and meaningful relationships with people you feel honored to be in a position to help. As an Advisor, you may well revel in your advisee's successes, but you do not lay claim to them.

<hr />

Cultivating dependence.

Every time an Advisor tells an advisee exactly what to do, they are, in effect, training the client to turn off their own discernment engines and put their faith entirely in the Advisor's judgment. Not only will the Advisor be wrong at times, this dynamic inevitably leaves advisees with less agency, less self-awareness, less self-confidence, less insight and without tools to make better decisions and create successful outcomes on their own. This may feel good to both parties in the beginning, especially if the advisee came to the Advisor in crisis, but it's a road to perpetual dependence, dysfunction, and limitation (and likely shame).

Advisors may well love working with certain people, but their primary job is to empower advisees with the support, insight, and frameworks to navigate better outcomes independently, even if they choose to keep the Advisor as a trusted confidante over time. Cultivating dependence not only risks disserving an advisee, it also can rise to the level, in extreme cases, of becoming predatory and inappropriate. Be mindful of supporting advisees as they learn to fish, rather than giving them the fish. Especially when the advisee is compensating the Advisor for services, which adds a layer of duty and complexity to the relationship.

Boundaries.

Advisors often become deeply attached to those they advise. This is to be expected, especially when you work with someone over a long window of time, and toward a highly personal and meaningful outcome. To the extent this helps provide the insight necessary to be more effective advisors, that's not a bad thing. But, without proper boundaries, it can lead to a level of clouded vision, emotional empathy, or transference that diminishes the objectivity needed to do the work you're there to do.

There will always come a time in the Advisor/advisee relationship where the Advisor needs to have a tough conversation in order to effectively do the work they've been tasked to do. The closer you are, the harder the hard conversations become and the greater the risk of ineffective or even harmful guidance that, inevitably, leads to the demise of the relationship.

Whenever possible in a professional setting, establish clear boundaries, be explicit, and even write them out and have all parties agree to abide by them. If the way you most often do the work of the Advisor is in a more personal, familiar context—parenting, supporting family or friends—this becomes a much more difficult proposition. Still, love and boundaries are not mutually exclusive. Love, in fact, is boundaries. Expectation setting is critical and gives you both the authority and permission to identify and address boundary crossings if and when they happen.

ADVISOR

SHOW ME THE MONEY.

Viewed as trusted guides and catalysts who accelerate outcomes and add value, often in measurable ways, capable Advisors tend to be highly sought after. Everyone wants them by their side, or in their organizations. That does not, however, always translate into high-level compensation.

In domains like business, competitive sport, and entertainment, the monetary rewards can be extraordinary, whether in a leadership role in an organization, consulting, coaching, or serving as an outside advisor. The same mix of insight and advisory ability is equally necessary everywhere from the nonprofit world to middle schools, to clergy, social work, or other domains where the rewards tend toward some blend of "livable" wage, along with the satisfaction of knowing you're doing the thing you're here to do and making a difference in the lives of people you truly care about. Then, there are myriad ways the Advisor can find an outlet in other parts of life, like parenting, being the wise aunt who guides her nieces, volunteering, coaching soccer on weekends, mentoring kids in the local community center, being an incredible friend, and more. In those realms, it's all about the feeling you get from doing the thing that fills your soul, while deepening into relationships with people you love to see lifted. Many Advisors find some blend of the above, focusing their advisory capabilities on business as a source of income, then complementing it in more personal, familial, or service-oriented ways in the evenings and on weekends. More on this in the "Spark Your Work" chapter.

No matter the area you choose to apply your impulse to advise, there will always be a similar limiting factor: experience and capability. It may take a significant amount of time before skill matches impulse on a level that leads to exceptional capability and, in turn, compensation or even the ability to help bring about genuinely valuable and reliable outcomes. This can be frustrating. It's important for rising Advisors to be patient. Do the work, build your wisdom and skills. Trust the process.

ADVISOR

THE
ADVOCATE
You, in a nutshell.

Animating impulse.

Advocates advocate, simple as that. It's all about shining the light, amplifying, and championing everything from an individual, community, or population to an idea, ideal, paradigm, institution, and beyond. This may involve literally "giving voice" to a person or cause that is, but for another's efforts, largely voiceless. Animals or the environment come to mind—they can't easily speak for themselves. Actually, they can (see barks and wildfires), but humans need to "translate" these signals into awareness, energy, agency, and action. Other times, it's less about giving voice and more about joining in an effort to champion and amplify an idea, need, point of view, voice, or community of voices. Being a part of that process makes you come alive. And, for most Advocates, it's been that way for as long as you can remember.

How that lands with those around you depends very much on the subject and the context. In one domain, it'll see the Advocate labeled a "born salesperson," champion for a noble cause, innovator, leader, or voice of a generation. Advocates who see the value of an ignored idea, then give it momentum, are often seen as visionaries. Those who shine the light on mistreatment or bullying, then stand up on behalf of others, are rewarded for not being bystanders. This same impulse, brought to bear in a different context, can find you labeled a rebel, change agent, rabble-rouser, dissident, or troublemaker. This is especially true when rebelling against the norms or rules of a household, organization, paradigm, culture, or institution where others are invested in the status quo.

Some Advocates feel called to particular subjects, people, or communities that they may be a part of, and go all in on those. Others are more broadly moved by a general sense of injustice in the face of power inequities and feel called to action, without a strong connection to the particular subject. Either way, you refuse to stand quiet in the face of any perceived idea, cause, or injustice that needs to be seen, heard, or championed. No matter how much caution or fear or concern may enter your consciousness, the bigger impulse to, as famed civil rights activist and congressman John Lewis offered, "make some noise and get in good trouble, necessary trouble" almost always pushes you forward. When it does, you come alive.

Megan.

A gifted therapist and teacher, Megan Devine (Advocate/Maven) lost her husband at a young age in a freak drowning accident. Devastated and searching for a way through, she found that her years of training and clinical experience, familiarity with the generations-old information, steps, and tropes around grief were not only woefully inadequate, but also potentially harmful. In fact, they often set unrealistic expectations that ended up layering shame and judgment on top of loss.

Looking to find a way back to a different kind of wholeness, she began to tap her Maven Shadow's impulse to learn and develop her own language, ideas, steps, and processes. What started as something deeply personal quickly became something bigger.

Megan's experience triggered her Advocate impulse to shine the light on a situation that needed to be changed. This was no longer just about her loss, it was about the ineffective practices and potential harm being done to millions who lose and grieve around the world. She began to offer her insights to a global community of people experiencing loss, founding the Refuge in Grief initiative that then spawned an achingly vast Writing Your Grief Community. Her book, *It's Okay That You're Not Okay*, followed a few years later, serving as a manifesto for a new approach to grief, and also for the dismantling of the old grief guard. You might look at Megan's experience and think she became an Advocate *because of* what happened to her. In fact, that is not the case. Megan's innate and, at times, consuming impulse to do the work of advocacy has been a part of her for as long as she can remember.

When Megan was in primary school, her class participated in an in-class craft and service fair called "integrity day." Kids made their own crafts, then sold them to teachers and other kids— everything from painted rocks to felt caterpillars.

In fourth grade, annoyed at something, maybe one of the kids, Megan's teacher announced he was canceling integrity day. Megan described what happened next, "after all the work the kids put in. Kids were mad. What did wee little powerhouse me do? Organized a strike and a march for our rights. We did the work. He removed the venue."

ADVOCATE

Standing up to anyone she perceived as a bully, personal or systemic, is what animated her from her earliest days. The impulse kept growing stronger with age. In her senior year of high school, then a cheerleader, Megan learned that the principal cut the cheering coach's pay, saying they couldn't afford it. She shared how the coach told the team, in tears. Megan marched into the principal's office, with her coach and the rest of the team, and grilled the principal, pushing him to, in her words, admit to all present that he cut the coach's salary because he didn't see them as real athletes, nor the coach as a "real" coach. She laid into him about the value the team and coach brought to the school, identifying tangible economic gain, and highlighting the importance of women in leadership positions.

Megan draws a direct line between moments like these and the grief work she does today, populated by countless additional moments along the way where she saw an injustice and stepped in to right it. Advocating has always been the thing she can't not do. Like all the Sparketypes, though it sometimes lies dormant for years or even decades, the impulse is pretty much always there, waiting for a reason, an invitation to take center stage.

The power of inciting incidents.

The Advocate's impulse is always there, though, for many, it remains somewhat quiet or simmering at a low burn in the background until something happens to trigger its emergence. Because of this, it may appear from the outside looking in that a particular moment turns someone into an Advocate when, in reality, they've always been one. It's just been stifled or under-expressed for any number of reasons, including safety, status, security, fear, anxiety, or the desire to keep harmony, belong, or maintain a certain benefit.

The triggering moment isn't as much about becoming as it is about activation or amplification. It awakens the impulse to step out of the shadow, or more fully into the light, and do the thing you're here to do. That moment or experience could be singular and personal, or it could be a series of experiences or a sustained pattern that impacts a wide swath of individuals, communities, or endeavors. Whatever the details, the moment or experience becomes an inciting incident. It triggers the Advocate's impulse to emerge on an entirely new level. When the subject is also deeply personal, it may well rise to the level of calling.

Deborah.

Deborah Owens (Advocate/Scientist) worked in sales, leadership, and development in the corporate world, eventually becoming the Director of Training for a large operating company owned by a global enterprise. Along the way, her sensibility was perpetually finding ways to shine the light on issues that not only mattered to her, but that she saw as critical to the growth of every employee and the organization, with a focus on equality, dignity, and respect. Fifteen years in, at the top of her career, Deborah landed in a position where, in addition to the heavy lifting she'd been doing around representation and equity for over a decade, she felt discriminated against and personally attacked on a level she hadn't experienced before. It went on for about eight months, with devastating physical and emotional consequences. Deborah eventually brought the situation to the president of the company, who immediately resolved it. While she stayed at the company, and took on increasingly powerful leadership roles, that moment awakened something in her. "I literally said to myself," she shared, "I don't want anybody else

ADVOCATE

to ever have to go through this. . . . It's so isolating. And so, I knew . . . then I was going to do everything in my power to make sure it didn't happen to other people."

That experience became an inciting incident to embrace advocacy around equity, race, and organizations in a more central way. Deborah eventually stepped away, took time for recuperation, reflection, and reimagination. Then, building around her Advocate's impulse, she launched her own consulting agency, Corporate Alley Cat, as a vehicle to champion equality and diversity within organizations, and also build and share tools and processes (her Scientist Shadow at work) to enable real, sustained change. "People were in pain . . . ," she offered, "and I came to believe that there was a reason why I had that experience. . . . I didn't know at that time. . . . But I felt like I had to do it not necessarily because I thought it would be fun. But . . . I knew people were in pain and I knew that people didn't understand that pain."

Many Advocates, at some point, experience an inciting incident or even a series of them that changes everything. These moments are catalytic. They channel the innate impulse to act, along with experience, insight, and capabilities, into a focal point—injustice or need for change—that is so deeply aligned with their values, experience, and beliefs that it sets them on a path that feels "bigger than them." They feel driven by not just a near-primal urge to champion and amplify, but also by a sense of responsibility to play a part, even if they're hesitant and there are many other things they could do. The inciting incident effectively gathers a more diffuse impulse to advocate, often spread across many moments and areas, into a laser-focused, values-fueled calling. When this happens, not only does the Advocate come most fully alive, but whatever it is they work to champion also benefits from the full weight of their gifts and efforts and the sense of devotion and conviction they radiate.

Building your own engine of change.

Many Advocates find themselves operating within the constraints and power dynamics of an existing relationship, family, community, organization, culture, paradigm, or group that they don't want to walk away from. They work to effect change from the inside out, leveraging the existing relationships, structures, resources, systems, social currency, and access to stakeholders to make a difference. Some big organizations even create the space for this, with time and resources specifically allocated for otherwise "indefensible" efforts. Google's 10 percent time comes to mind. Others, though, especially those whose Advocate Primary pairs with a Maker or Scientist Shadow, may be more inclined to not only argue for a better and different future, but also to step away from all the good and bad of the existing dynamic or system and build something entirely new that solves the problem in the way they most want it solved.

Linda.

Linda Buchner (Advocate/Advisor) spent the first twenty-five years of her career in the world of advertising and marketing, spotlighting the stories of organizations, products, and people in nearly every channel possible. She was accomplished, at the top of her field. But as she entered the middle season of life, her Advocate impulse began to pull her in a different direction. She wanted to devote her energy, along with the incredible skillset she'd developed, to something that made a real difference. She wanted her life to "mean something" beyond the constraints of her current job. So, she refocused her lens on community and impact.

Linda also wanted more control over the projects and people she supported, so she launched her own consulting practice

ADVOCATE

with a focus on cause marketing for nonprofit organizations. She loved bringing together different stakeholders and working to tell the collective story in a way where everyone rose together. At a certain point, Linda felt called to take an even bigger step — she didn't just want to advocate for a solution, she wanted to help create it.

Linda had been working with organizations in community education. She saw firsthand how certain people just weren't well served by the existing paradigm. So, she helped to bring together a team to create a Saturday program called Minddrive that focused on experiential learning. Every week, a group of mentors would gather as a team and work with students to build an electric car from scratch. Along the way, they'd learn everything they needed, from math to science, design to communications, and collaboration. Linda led everything from fundraising to teaching students about PR, storytelling, speaking, and beyond. While she's since stepped away from that endeavor, she continues to work in a hands-on way with organizations to help raise funds and also advise (her Shadow) on the creation of impact-driven programs and solutions.

Evan.

Evan LaRuffa (Advocate/Maven), founder of arts-education initiative I Paint My Mind, shares a similar impulse to not just call for change, but be the change. He sees the experience of beauty, provocation, emotion, expression, and the sense of connectedness and possibility that comes from both experiencing and creating art as fundamental to human flourishing. To him, limiting artistic enjoyment and expression to only a small number of people causes harm not only to all the individuals who've been excluded from the experience, but to society writ large. Art, in his heart and mind, is a human right. This is the ideal that animates his Advocate's impulse.

Rather than work within the constraints of the existing gallery or educational systems, he created his own innovative model, founding the public art and education initiative I Paint My Mind (IPMM). Their mission is to "transform people and spaces through the power of art . . . by connecting artists, business, and communities to mobilize a wheel of impact that creates value and access."

IPMM's approach is radical, and it works. The foundation buys art from local, underrepresented artists. This allows them to support the creators, while curating and building a sizable collection they then sell to collectors or lease to large organizations for display in their offices.

A portion of the contributions from client organizations and collectors circles back to fund sustained art purchases and also bring art to underserved communities, public spaces, and schools through IPMM's Shared Walls™ initiative. Another portion pays for the continued development of a robust K–12 art curriculum that is distributed to teachers and schools at a time where art isn't just missing from the walls of classrooms, but is being stripped from instructional offerings as well.

For Evan, it's not just about art; it's about equity and social justice. It's about correcting for the fact that schools in certain places are underfunded, making the enjoyment and expression of art unavailable. With IPMM, he hasn't just created a vehicle to advocate for the enjoyment and creation of art in underserved communities, he's built an alternate ecosystem that supports artists, organizations, teachers, schools, students, and communities in a way that simply did not exist before.

ADVOCATE

The introverted Advocate.

Similar to Warriors, Advocates often feel bound by a certain so-cietal assumption that, to do their work, they must be forward-facing, loud, raging extroverts. It's not just about *holding* a mega-phone, it's about *being* one. That works for some. Fact is, many of the greatest Advocates and change-makers in history, art, sci-ence, government, faith, and life either pulse between extreme exposure and complete cloistering or they do their work from a quieter, more introverted, sensitive, collaborative, internal place. They figure out ways to accomplish what they need, but also honor their social wiring so they don't end up perpetually empty and, eventually, physically and emotionally unwell.

Glennon.

Love Warrior and *Untamed* author Glennon Doyle is the founder of social-change movement and foundation Together Rising. Through her organizations and social accounts, Glennon teams with other leaders and activists to rally what she describes as Love Flash Mobs, mobilizing millions of people to come to-gether and support specific causes. When these campaigns are active, Glennon is fiercely public and engaged, amplifying the cause. She's everywhere, front and center, sharing, interacting, leading. She would appear, at first glance, to be a raging extro-vert. In truth, she's the exact opposite.

Glennon has learned to take on the role of Advocate in a way that allows her to honor her inner introvert and take care of herself (though, that is a fairly regular struggle). Much of her work is accomplished from home, behind a screen, sharing im-ages, videos, captions, and organizing other leaders, influencers, and supporters to share the message and rally their communi-ties behind the scenes and screens. When she speaks, she also knows she needs to retreat to recover, or else she won't have the reserves needed to do the hard work of making change. She steps away when she needs, to be with her wife, family, and dogs and to take care of herself. Still, the impact has been stunning.

When it comes to expressing your Advocate's impulse, you do not have to buy into anyone else's proclamation of the "right" way to do it. If you feel energized operating in an extroverted mode, and that is sustainable, have at it. If not, if you're called to the work of the Advocate, but are also wired socially in a much more introverted way, honor that as well.

Tap technology to find the sweet spot between impact, expression, and sustainable effort. Invest your efforts in quieter, more intimate, yet equally important and impact-creating conversations, negotiations, introductions, and other interactions that let you feel fully expressed. Look, also, at your Shadow Sparketype for hints about channels and outlets. Make art or music (Maker), solve complex problems (Scientist), become encyclopedic on the root cause of the problem (Maven) so you can share your wisdom with fellow Advocates, create systems and processes (Essentialist) that get more done with less effort. You get the point. Whatever you do, if you are an Advocate who is also introverted, do not let your social wiring get in the way of your impulse to make a difference.

WHAT TRIPS YOU UP.

Advocates are often fierce in their will, their hearts, and their actions. This is one of the qualities that allows them to be effective at the work of advocacy, but it can also trip them up in different ways. A large part of their work involves identifying and feeling the weight of inequity, even if that is simply the

ADVOCATE

observation that there's a better way to do something. That, alone, can be hard, especially if they or their ideas and ideals are simultaneously bearing the burden and force of the harm. Layered onto this is the call and the effort needed to champion and amplify, to lead and sometimes build or be the change. Shifting people's attention and beliefs, changing ideas, structures, stories, and paradigms, can become a pretty heavy lift and certain dynamics can add to that effort. It's helpful to have a sense for the common experiences that are likely to drop into the path, so you can be better equipped to handle them, if and when they do.

Lack of control.

Advocates tend to be pretty single-minded in their beliefs and approaches. Because of this, decision by committee, endless conversation and inaction, rather than decisiveness and coherent action, can be difficult for Advocates to deal with. When advocating in a high-stakes, dogmatic, inflexible, or complex dynamic, this nearly always becomes an issue, especially when you see current harm happening and time is of the essence. Similarly, having little control over the resources needed to stand for those you're representing, or not having enough control over the call to action, process, or outcome, can be incredibly frustrating. This is a challenge not just for young advocates, but even for many experienced Advocates who operate within organizations or systems that are perpetually underresourced, disenfranchised, or ignored.

Stephen.

Stephen Haff (Advocate/Nurturer) was a New York City public high school teacher in Brownsville, Brooklyn. He struggled on nearly every level in the early days, working within a system that seemed built more around order and control than growth. Trying to create and maintain a safe environment and inspire students to show up for class, participate, engage with the work, and share their experiences was a perpetual losing battle. It was incredibly frustrating. He received little support from colleagues and administrators when proposing alternative ideas, not because they didn't care, but because they were grappling with the same limitations and lack of support and control. His students weren't learning. The one thing Stephen was there to do simply wasn't happening.

One day, he brought blank journals into his class, handed one to each student, and invited them to write anything they wanted to him and he promised to write back. Every day, they'd turn in books filled with writing and images from the night before. He'd take them home and write back. He was building trust, getting to know his students and showing them he cared. The experience was transformative, but it also took many hours every night. Added to the already heavy workload of teaching in public school, reading and responding thoughtfully to dozens of students, many in dire need, pushed him to the brink of mental illness. He had what he describes as a breakdown. In order to reclaim his own mental health, he stepped away from teaching, but he never stopped thinking about how to better serve kids.

A few years later, in a much better place, he began to rebuild on his own terms. He wanted to continue to champion and uplift the most underserved students in the neighborhood, often the young children of immigrants. He knew they could not pay him, so he began simply by putting the word out in the neighborhood that he'd teach reading and writing once a week in a local pizza place, for free. There was only one rule: Everyone listens to everyone. Everyone has a voice. He created a container

ADVOCATE

for each child to be heard, to advocate for themselves. Kids of all ages began to come. In short order, his project outgrew the pizza place and he started to attract the attention of believers in his work who became patrons and allowed him to open his own one-room schoolhouse.

The kids came up with the name Still Waters in a Storm, a nod to the safe place he provided to not just learn and grow and feel safe sharing your work, but to belong. When met with a stifling lack of control over his ability to the thing he was wired to do, Stephen created an entirely new paradigm for learning that not only served as an outlet for his deep desire to teach, but also championed the kids yearning to be seen, heard, learn, and grow.

———

Nothing is truly binary.

Beyond being single-minded, Advocates may also tend toward binary thinking, looking at everyone else and thinking, "You're either for this, or against it." Problem is, rarely is that reality. Part of the work of the Advocate is to step into moments, circumstances, relationships, and interactions understanding that few things are truly binary. Everything from beliefs and identity to alliances and actions lies on a spectrum. The question is never, "Are you with us, or against us?" but rather, "Is there some way to do this dance where we both can win?"

A counterintuitive quirk of advocacy is that the most effective Advocates are often not the loudest or most dug in, but rather the ones who invite nuance and understanding in the name of movement and transformation.

———

Trystan.

Trystan Angel Reese is a husband, father, trans-man, and advocate for equality. When he and his husband decided to share his story of becoming pregnant, the internet as well as many in the "real" world did not respond kindly. People denied not just his right to exist, but his very existence. For years before, Trystan had worked as an Advocate for LGBTQIA+ rights in the field, knocking on doors with the intention of first creating safety and understanding, then, if possible, support for policy changes aimed at equality.

His approach was based on a studied and proven process of conversation that opens the door to understanding and, potentially, change that many political canvassers and advocates are schooled in. It is also remarkably similar to the methods embraced by many of the most effective salespeople in business. It started with curiosity and empathy, then led to commonality, and, when the opportunity presented itself, openness to a new point of view.

There were some people, he learned, who were so dug in that a civil and open conversation wasn't possible. Others, though, started out having seen both Trystan and the world he represented differently, but were cautiously open to learning more and even welcomed the chance to have a better understanding of the issues, of him, and of what was really at stake.

Starting from a place of openness, commonality, and seeing people not in a binary way but rather on a spectrum of understanding and potential for mutual understanding, connection, and, potentially, allyship set the tone for the possibility of sustained change.

Trystan, who was called to do this work, made it not just his occupation, but also his vocation, and was willing to take on the burden of advocating for change. That said, when the person

ADVOCATE

doing the work of advocacy or persuasion is also the person suffering harm at the hand of those very people, systems, or paradigms, directly or indirectly, doing the work of understanding, empathizing with, and moving them into your corner can be experienced as a piling on of a burden that unfairly layers even more work onto the psyche of the very people who are already bearing too much.

Who bears the burden of advocacy?

Whether arguing for an idea or championing a team around a conference table, or pushing forward a law that acknowledges equality and protection for a community that has been disenfranchised, or leading a community or team, advocacy takes work. Often, tremendous amounts of labor, resources, sacrifice, and emotion over a long period of time.

Question is, who most often bears that burden? And who *should* bear it?

Answer is, it's complicated.

Advocacy begins by drawing attention, then moves into persuasion, and finally calls for an action. As a general principle, in personal relationships, in business, and in life, the burden of persuasion goes to the persuader. People generally won't sell themselves a new set of beliefs, behaviors, actions, products, solutions, or things when the ones they have give them a certain amount of comfort. We accept that when it comes to selling a car, pitching an idea or project in a work context, asking for a raise, advocating for how you're a good fit for a job, college, client, or worthy of a loan. But when we zoom the lens out to broader, more pervasive social issues, things change. The "general principles" tend to fall apart, where equity demands a more nuanced examination of the burden of advocacy, especially the educational lift, emotional labor, and compassion that are often an expected part of it.

What if the circumstances that lead to advocacy involved people, communities, or populations who are, in this very moment, facing insurmountable challenges? What if the Advocate is one of those people? What if they are a part of a larger community who are all experiencing a similar, present harm, and the change they're advocating for requires those who are either actively causing or complicit in the harm to change their beliefs and actions? Who bears the burden of advocacy and persuasion then? Is it right to *expect* any individual or community who has been harmed or is being harmed to then undertake the work needed to convince those causing them pain to stop?

Short answer, no. It is not their job to walk another through a process of awakening to the harm they are either directly causing or turning a blind eye to, and even benefiting from. It is relentlessly, exhaustingly wrong. And yet, it is so often what is asked and expected across a wide variety of contexts.

For many Advocates, progress is a dirty word.

Building on a binary lens, there may be a tendency for Advocates to see progress in a very binary way as well. Outcomes that do not meet every expectation are viewed as outright failures. Part of the work of the Advocate is to cultivate the openness and ability to discern when good enough is truly not good enough, or when it's a sign of progress and, while the ultimate outcome may still lie ahead, it's okay to take pride and satisfaction in the steps along the way. This is true whether you're arguing for a policy change at work that leads, instead, to a working paper or committee, selling an enterprise-wide system upgrade to a client that ends with a more modest incremental update, or pitching an investor on an idea that leads to a follow-up meeting with the full board, rather than the desired term sheet and check.

At the end of the day, the best an Advocate can do is the best they can do. That sometimes means the thing they were striving for wasn't accomplished. It's okay to feel discontent and even grief. But in the context of the opportunity to do what you do to the best of your ability, if you know, deep down, you've shown up and given everything you had to give, you can and should still open to the peace of mind in knowing you've spent your time doing the thing you're here to do, and done it to the best of your abilities. You may not have accomplished the full list of things, but, especially when you're advocating for complex, long-standing change, every step forward matters.

Part of the challenge and the work of being an Advocate is being able to discern the difference between aligned action and successful outcome. Each contributes to your ability to come fully alive. It's never entirely about the outcome, but rather how you've brought yourself to the work, who or what you've lifted up along the way, and whether the needle has moved, even if not all the way.

When giving everything leaves you with nothing.

Last thing, Advocates, as we know, are fierce. Even when they're quieter, more introverted in approach. Even though doing the thing you're here to do gives you energy, changing beliefs and championing outcomes can be incredibly hard work. Ferocity takes energy. In fact, depending on how personally connected you are to the focus of your advocacy, it can become all-consuming.

Sometimes, the combination of effort and high stakes can leave you emotionally, psychologically, and physically drained. It is critically important to create mechanisms to check in on your state of being, and cultivate practices that allow you to regularly refill your tank. If you're falling apart, it becomes brutally hard for you to do the work you're here to do. This is not just about Advocates who are called to vast, complex systemic issues. It can show up in any domain, personal or professional, where the impulse is expressed in the context of work that is, by its very nature, deeply emotional, high-stakes, and stressful.

Michelle.

Emergency medicine doctor Michele Harper (Advocate/Warrior) steps into people's lives at moments of dire need, helps them heal, and gives them hope. Completing her residency, she chose to serve underresourced hospitals in underserved communities. As a Black woman in the practice of medicine, Michele was already acutely aware of the chasm in representation in the profession and how that affects not only the standard of care given to the mostly Black and Brown communities she served, but also the standard of dignity and safety afforded to her and her colleagues.

For Michele, the decision to pursue medicine wasn't just about healing, it was about justice. She wants to be in a place where she can champion equal access to care and ensure her patients are being seen, heard, responded to, and provided equal treatment by healthcare professionals. She calls attention to the need for change, and leads and participates in actually *being* the change on a lived, daily basis.

In her bestselling memoir, *The Beauty of Breaking*, Michele shared many of the ways these inequities show up. Doing this work is her calling, but it is also, at times, a psychologically and

ADVOCATE

physically grueling way to serve. When the pandemic hit, extreme illness amplified the inequity, while also pushing her and her colleagues to the brink, with unforgiving hours, exposure to illness, and utter exhaustion. This reinforced the lessons Michele had already begun to understand about self-care and advocacy. If you want to be in a position to serve, you need to also cultivate the practices that give you the equanimity, energy, vitality, and presence of mind that sustains you through the often challenging experience of working for some greater ideal or good. Her commitment to her patients, colleagues, and community required her to double down on her commitment to her own well-being as a key element of her ability to keep doing the work she's here to do.

SHOW ME THE MONEY.

For some, there's a fairly conventional, obvious path to monetizing or earning a living that not only allows you to express your inner Advocate, but even requires it. Jobs like lawyers, lobbyists, salespeople, public or patient advocates, speakers, evangelists, spokespeople, aid-workers, ambassadors, and more come to mind. Less obvious, though, is the fact that the ability to champion, amplify, and persuade is of tremendous value in nearly any setting, role, or organization. In nearly every domain, ideas, solutions, people, stakeholders, communities, projects, and ideals all need attention, power, and momentum. Many fields value this ability and compensate it well.

An essential element of advocacy is representation and persuasion. Advocates are effectively drawing your attention to, then selling, an idea, ideal, a mechanism, or outcome — often one that requires not just an opening of the mind, but sometimes

ADVOCATE

even a deeper shift in beliefs that lead to action. That capability is valued in nearly every domain. It does not matter if you call yourself an Advocate or activist or champion, an agent, leader, publicist, editor, producer, journalist, or any other role. As with every Sparketype, titles are largely irrelevant. It's about the impulse that drives you and the opportunity to bring it to bear. Many of those opportunities show up in realms that are tethered not just to the chance to shine a light and make a difference, but also create a very nice living. Even if you've not yet found a specific focus that aligns the impulse with a deep interest that translates to a sense of calling, the simple opportunity to exercise the impulse on a regular basis can be incredibly nourishing.

That said, there may be times when the impulse finds its most personal and compelling outlet in an idea, person, community, or ideal that does not have an easy, conventional connection to a sustainable income. Maybe you feel called to champion the creation or maintenance of a local garden or, on a larger scale, preservation of the Amazon forest or national parks. You might feel called to activism or even volunteering at a local hospice to help humanize end-of-life care for people in underresourced communities.

Some of this work may be sustainable through positions at private or nonprofit organizations, grants, or other contributions. Sometimes, you'll be able to figure out ways to create your own funding mechanisms or solutions that others might pay for. Sponsorship, fundraising, or foundations can serve as ways for those who share your values and beliefs to get behind your effort. Other times, however, this work may not have any ready or easy path to money. Even though it is deeply of service, needed, and valued. In those moments, Advocates may need to make decisions about how much of their impulse will be devoted in a particular way simply because it's the thing they can't *not* do,

ADVOCATE

regardless of any ability to generate a sustainable living, versus the need or value-based drive for financial comfort and security that may come from its application in a field with a clearer path to compensation.

Either way, it is brutally hard for Advocates to completely stifle the impulse. Whether it is the central devotion and prime source of income, something you do in exchange for less-than-complete compensation, the thing you do because you are called to do it, or some blend, be sure to create ways for the impulse to be expressed. The longer it stays bottled up inside, the more harm you end up doing to yourself.

THE
NURTURER
You, in a nutshell.

I've got you.

Animating impulse.

Nurturers nurture. They give care, take care, offer support, see you, hear you, hold you. They help lift you up and walk beside you when you need them. They help when you're going through something (which, at times, is entire seasons of life). They see and often feel unease, pain, and suffering in others, and seek to ease it in a very personal, hands-on way, not because they're paid to do it (though that may be the case), but because they can't not do it.

This Sparketype, in fact, often finds a powerful outlet in non-professional pursuits, expressed as a desire to help friends, strangers, animals, or even entire populations or ecosystems whose pain they simply cannot witness without doing something about it. When they have the opportunity to give care, and witness or even share in the difference it makes, even if they're never directly thanked, they take refuge and deep satisfaction in knowing they've done what they've come to do.

Nurturers also tend to be deeply empathic. For many, they've been this way as long as they can remember. Sometimes to their detriment, they feel others' unease, pain, or suffering on a level that paralyzes, rather than mobilizes them. They see others in need and feel called to help, in whatever way they can, sometimes to the point where they give so much, there's nothing left for them.

For some Nurturers, the call is connected to a single being, living thing, or discrete group, community, or population. This might range from an aging relative to a child in need, an animal at a shelter, or an ancient forest. For others, the yearning to give care and uplift is felt more broadly. Anyone or anything that is in need becomes an anchor for their impulse. And anything that gets in the way becomes a source of pain or, for some, a trigger for a more creative approach. What most Nurturers eventually discover, however, is their most valued offering isn't their world or actions, but simply their presence, devotion, and attention. Nurturers see you, hold you up, and let you know you're not alone.

Jen.

On the inside of Jen Pastiloff's (Nurturer/Sage) left forearm, a few inches up from her wrist, is a tattoo. Three simple words in black ink, "I got you." The moment you meet her, you realize she does. Simply because you're alive. There's nothing you need to do, or be, or become. The fact of your existence gives you a place in her heart.

For as long as she can remember, Jen has felt what those around her feel. That can be a great thing. It allows her to participate in their successes as if they're her own, and sense when and how to be there when they need help. It can also be a hard thing. She feels their pain, often, as if it were hers.

When Jen looks at you, she sees all of you. Into you. And through you. She wants to know what's under the surface. Behind your eyes, in your heart. For years, she waited tables in Los Angeles to pay the bills while trying to break into the entertainment business. The break never came, but her customers loved her, and felt loved by her. She was always leaning in to not just hear their orders, but share in the moments of their lives. She cared deeply, but there was something else, another reason Jen would drop down to their level and ease in close.

Jen is deaf. She wants to see you, get close to you, in part, so she can hear you with her eyes and her aids, and feel you. Her customers never knew. It happened slowly, over time. She kept telling herself it wasn't happening, until she couldn't. Over the years, Jen taught herself to read lips as a way to stay connected to a world that grew quieter by the day. Turns out, this capacity, the ability to hyper-focus her attention and intention, to not just see words, but also take in gestures, emotions, and energy, though honed in the kitchens and chaos of L.A., has become more than just a survival mechanism or mode of communication. It's a bit of a Nurturer superpower, a two-way tie-line between her heart-centered soul and anyone fortunate enough to get lost in the spell her presence casts. To be held by her gaze is, simply, to be held.

Now years into an ever-evolving journey that found her leaving the restaurant, getting married, having a son, then taking her seat as a teacher, mentor, and coach (her Shadow is the Sage; she illuminates, in no small part to elevate), Jen has focused her intentions and effort largely on the community of women, often moving through the middle season of life. She leads workshops and international retreats on meditation, presence, surrender, creativity, writing, and freedom. Her first book, *On Being Human: A Memoir of Waking Up, Living Real, and Listening Hard*, was a moving Nurturer's offering, layered not just with story, but insights that allowed readers to explore their own path to reawakening. Jen's hugs and laughs and words leave you wiser. But, at the end of the day, it's her capacity and commitment to see you, really see you, to let you feel held and valued, that not only leaves you lifted, but allows both you and her to come most fully alive. If you ask Jen why she's here on the planet, her answer is simple. "At the end of my life, when I say one final *What have I done?* let my answer be, *I have done love.*"

Finding your unique expression.

Like Jen, some Nurturers are called to care for pretty much anyone who's going through anything. While her focus over this season of life has narrowed a bit to a community of women navigating the middle years of life, she feels unease and suffering in nearly every interaction with the world around her, and is compelled to help, often lifting up total strangers in a moment of need. Others may find themselves with a direct empathic connection with and desire to serve a particular person, being, or community and not feel overly affected or strongly called by any other need. The impulse, it seems, can be either broad in scope or highly selective. Still others feel called to step in at a particular moment in time, where they feel they can be most useful, and make the biggest difference, or some blend of the above.

Chris.

Barefoot Rehabilitation Clinic founder Chris Stepien (Nurturer/Scientist) was trained, originally, as a chiropractor, though his

NURTURER

skill set and experience have expanded over decades into a multimodal approach to treating pain. He is unique in his abilities, and deeply empathic. He feels everything, from everyone. For years, that showed up as a general impulse to take on others' pain, no matter who or how or when. But with intention, Chris has narrowed his focus to take care of a very specific person, in a very specific way, at a very specific moment in time. At his clinics, there is a screening process before being accepted as a patient. Among other criteria, an individual must be experiencing chronic pain, have already tried to resolve it, and failed with at least three other professionals. Chris wants the hardest cases, the ones mapped by the type of pain that makes most other healing professionals throw up their hands in exasperation.

In the beginning, when he was grappling with his own awakening and struggling with depression, working with patients in dire straits was the thing that was meaningful enough to get him out of bed. Now, coming from a more healed place himself, this calling is driven more by a desire to serve at the moment of greatest need, where he can make the biggest difference. It is both a reflection of his Nurturer impulse being called into action in a very specific way, and his Scientist Shadow seeking the challenge of figuring out the most complex cases.

Still, having now learned how to do the thing he's here to do in a way that allows him to remain healthy along the way, before taking on a client, there is a final question. Wrapping the initial consult, he'll ask, "Have you suffered enough yet?" He's not being glib. He simply wants to know you're ready to let go of your pain. Nothing he does, he's learned, can help if you're not ready to surrender what, for many, has become the most intimate relationship in their lives. He's not afraid of hard cases. He just wants to know that, if he says yes and devotes himself to your healing, you're ready to be there with him. That's part of how he stands fully in his Nurturer role, helping walk people through and away from pain, while protecting himself from his own suffering along the way and allowing his impulse the ability to become fully expressed.

Nurturers often do their work in nontraditional ways.

When you think about Nurturers, there's often an assumption that they're limited to certain roles, where giving or taking care is front and center in the job description. There's a tendency to conjure this image of a perpetually smiling walking hug in a fleece track suit with comfortable shoes, just meandering around and being lovey-dovey to all. That may be the case for some, but it need not be. The impulse often finds a powerful outlet in the context of jobs, roles, or careers that would greatly benefit from it, yet may not explicitly ask for or require it. And it may show up in people who feel the impulse to lift others up, yet don't feel the need to do it in a way most others might predict.

Teri.

Teri Pruitt (Nurturer/Maven) found an outlet for her Nurturer impulse in a very specific and unique way. For her, it's less about relieving suffering, and more about creating a ripple of care and elevation. Teri is a dresser on Broadway. She works with actors in the casts of many of the biggest shows on theater's grandest avenue, most recently in the show *Wicked*.

From her title, you might think actors just show up, have Teri help them on with their costumes, then rush off to hair and makeup and hit the stage. The truth is anything but. Teri's relationship with her actors is sacred. They are, as she relayed, "my" actors. Not in a possessive sense, but in a devotional sense. Teri is care person zero in the community of performers, crew, backstage, and front-of-the-house. She's the one who welcomes her performers "home" every day, invites them in, and learns everything she can to make them feel safe, cozy, centered, seen, and completely wrapped in love and care. She lives and serves at the sweet spot of exquisite attention and generosity of spirit, doing everything she can to allow them to be at their best when it matters most.

If an actor shares a preference for honey in her jasmine tea, she will never have to ask again, it's just there. One actor may prefer fun banter, another quiet reflection. Neither has to tell Teri; she notices their preference and, in every interaction thereafter, honors it. As a dresser, she doesn't just help with costumes, she helps her people step into a character or role or mode of being. Touch is a big part of her work. With what she does, it must be. There, again, she observes how people respond, being more physical when it's received as nourishment, and less when not. In her mind, she is there to offer acts of service that let people know they are seen, they matter, they are known and cared for.

Interestingly, while Teri's focus in entirely on her actors in the moment, she is also aware of the potential great theater holds to set in motion a bigger ripple of care, and the part she plays in it. She takes care of her actors, who in turn take care of the story, which when delivered by a cast and crew who are at their best, creates a moment of transcendence, awakening, and revelation for the audience. A dollop of raw Manuka honey in a favorite mug of jasmine tea is the drop in the pond that leaves the couple in the third-to-last row in the second mezzanine broken open in the best of ways.

That is her devotion, her contribution, her nourishment and salvation.

It's not always a huggy thing.

Hearing the stories above, you might guess all Nurturers are warm and fuzzy, heart-on-their-sleeve people, destined to find their ways into traditional helping professions. Many do, but just because this is an obvious path doesn't mean Nurturers are limited to it. Nor does it mean all Nurturers are emotionally effusive, touchy-feely borderline (or full-on) hippies. As with all of the Sparketypes, their ability to offer empathy, compassion, and elevation crosses nearly every field, industry, or title. What's paramount and consistent across every channel of expression is a commitment to the relationship, to creating a deep and enduring sense of trust, safety, and, at times, love, in support of the way you serve. In fact, a healthy part of the benefit Nurturers provide is derived not only from what they do, but also from who they are, how present they can be, and how genuine and enduring their relationship becomes. These qualities are equally at home in the therapist's office and the conference table.

Sarah.

Sarah Geddess (Nurturer/Advocate) runs Calgary-based communications agency Press + Post. Their focus is public relations with a specialization in crisis preparation and management, serving mostly small businesses and entrepreneurs. Her job is to take care of her clients through the wildly uncertain swings of building a company and the crises that, for many, are always just around the corner. It's not a matter of if, but rather when and how.

It's easy to see how her Nurturer/Advocate aligns well with this work. When things get volatile and founders and teams feel like their worlds are spinning out of control, having someone with both the skill to walk you through it and advocate on your

NURTURER

behalf, as well as the impulse to take care of you every step of the way, is a good thing. Sarah takes it a step further. Over the years, she's learned that the pain of dealing with a crisis when you're in it is much lower if you've already anticipated and prepared for it in advance. So, her nurturing has taken on more of a preemptive approach.

She works with founders and teams to identify everything that could implode, describe their nightmare meltdown in all its glory, the worst-case scenario, even if the likelihood of it ever happening is slim. It might seem counterintuitive to do this. Wouldn't that effectively be causing her clients to drop into a place of angst and suffering that may never become their reality? Nurturing is supposed to be about the opposite, right? Removing pain, not causing it! Not so fast.

Once Sarah has identified and walked a client through their worst-case scenario, she works with them to develop a preemptive strategic plan. This becomes a road map that details exactly what to do, the step-by-step actions, resources, and messaging, and shows them how, even in crisis, they'd be okay. The process itself can be anxiety-inducing, but the outcome lets them breathe easier knowing, if the worst happens, they know what to do, and they have someone they trust that'll be by their side. It's one of the ways she makes them feel taken care of, which has always been her leading impulse. It's not so much a touchy-feely way of nurturing, but rather a confident, grounding presence coupled with a wise skills approach to tapping her Nurturer. Being able to serve on that level is what Sparks her.

Billy.

Billy Michels (Nurturer/Sage) found an outlet for his Nurturer's impulse in photography. When Billy's dad, who was a legendary storyteller, died a few years back, Billy realized he had no video

NURTURER

of him. Which deepened his sense of grief and loss. Building on what had been a side-passion for photography and videography, his Nurturer side wondered how many others felt this same sense of loss. He wanted to help, so he started a photography and video project called ShineLight Legacy that produces documentary-style videos as tributes, reflections, and keepsakes. He not only wants to create a video that gives continued comfort, he also wants those participating in it to feel seen, heard, and cared for throughout the process of creation. While growing this same venture, Billy found himself facing a diagnosis of stage-4 cancer. Now healthy, the experience transformed his approach to work, life, relationships, and his own sense of legacy. In addition to his work on ShineLight Legacy, he now integrates his Sage Shadow to teach others how he approached his own healing journey, so that others might learn from and be comforted by his insights.

Nurturing truly does take every form and finds a path of expression in nearly every domain of work and life. Our work is to embrace it and find the way to build upon it, so that we can step more fully into ourselves and feel more fully alive.

WHAT TRIPS YOU UP.

While Nurturers are wired to make an incredible difference in people's lives, whether in an intimate, personal way or even at scale in a large, organizational way, as with all Sparketypes, there is a fairly common set of challenges Nurturers tend to bump up against. Knowing these possible stumbling points in advance might help you become more aware of when you're heading toward one so you can avoid it. And understanding what's really happening, coupled with the knowledge that you're not alone, can help you figure out how to move through it and return to a place of more healthy and constructive nurturing with greater speed and ease. Here are some of the most common stumbling points and triggers.

Becoming "one" with those you serve.

There's a common phenomenon shared by Nurturers. Because many Nurturers are highly empathic—they feel what others feel, both the good and the bad—they often experience a sense of merging with those they seek to serve. This can be an incredible blessing, when you're all moving into a better, more elevated place together. It can also become a source of struggle and emptiness. Sometimes, it's both at once.

Agapi.

Agapi Stassinopoulos is pure love. Her name literally translates to *love*. The first time I met her, she was a guest on the *Good Life Project* podcast. I opened the door to find her, glowing and smiling, and holding a large box filled with Greek pastries. The moment the box left her hands, I was wrapped in a hug. We'd never met, yet to her, we were already family. Agapi cannot help but to radiate what she calls her Agapiness through everything from bestselling books to workshops, keynotes, meditations, performances, and beyond. "I always had this sense of oneness," she shared. "My heart touches to people. I've had it since I was a little girl. I see into other people's hearts." This capacity for empathy and desire to lift the spirits of others allows her to experience a sense of merging. "The minute I step onstage, my energy expands." Agapi adds, "I become total oneness with others. No self-consciousness. No separation. Complete absorption.

It is spiritual in its convergence of the physical and spiritual. It's like having a group orgasm; you melt with everyone in the room. The ultimate goal is to create the experience of union in love, to become and radiate love and have everyone feel love and be love." This sense of oneness can be transcendent in its ability to connect with and elevate individuals and groups. But it also comes with a dark side.

To become a part of a collective human organism, even for a moment, is to share in its joy, and its sorrow. Agapi is such a deep empath, so drawn to wanting others to feel held, it can become overwhelming. The conduit that allows her to feel others' suffering, then lift them into love, also delivers their darkness to her doorstep. Over time, Agapi learned that she had to develop clear boundaries and adopt self-care practices that would allow her to continue to do the work of the Nurturer, to merge and rise when possible, but also remove herself from the often perilous cliff of emotional empathy when it became clear that a complete merging would help neither the people she sought to serve nor her.

She also realized she had to let go of her own attachment to wanting others to feel and be better, to allow them to feel what they needed to feel, and be there for them in whatever capacity they were open to. "I had to learn," she said, "that just cultivating my own Agapiness, my own ability to be and radiate love, then be in communion with people, would be enough."

> You don't have to "take on" others'
> pain in order to lift them up.

Remember pain-doc Chris Stepien (Nurturer/Scientist)? There must be something about tattoos and Nurturers. Scribed across the knuckles of Chris's left hand is the word L-O-V-E. This makes perfect sense, given the healer he's become, but there's a very different reason those letters sit where he can see them all day, every day. "You can't have LOVE tattooed on your fingers," he told me, "and be an asshole."

When Chris was in high school, he was obsessed with football. He played an incredibly violent game. He'd take great pleasure in annihilating any opponent who dared to get close to a teammate. That same simmering aggression came out over the years in the form of harm not just toward others, but also toward himself. He'd regularly put himself in the path of violence. Yes, we're talking about the same person who pursued a degree in chiropractic medicine and rapidly built a packed private practice that focused on relieving pain and empowering patients with the practices needed to remain pain-free.

How could this be the same person who led with such aggression earlier in life? That very question led Chris into years of self-discovery and inner work. Turns out, there was a bit of a hidden script running that is not uncommon in Nurturers, and that, once revealed, would illuminate and reframe this experience in the language of caregiving. Beyond past experiences he needed to process, there was another story he'd been unwittingly living his whole life that was closely tied to his Nurturer impulse. His calling to remove other people's suffering had tied itself to the false notion that, for them to be okay, he had to sacrifice himself in some way. Their pain had to become his; he had to preemptively take it on, so they'd never feel it or so they could release it into him. On the football field as a kid, what looked like aggression toward an opponent was really a relentless drive to protect and take care of the people he loved from relative strangers. He'd regularly sacrifice his own body in the name of saving them.

NURTURER

Once he was able to uncross these wires and realize he didn't need to take on another's pain in order to relieve them of it or preempt them from it, everything began to change. He was able to grow into his professional practice in a much healthier way, building his own self-healing and self-love practice along the way. He got that LOVE tattoo on his left hand because he didn't always like the way he acted toward himself and others, and wanted a visual reminder to come back to kindness. Now, years later, it's become more of a gentle reminder not just of who he has become, how he aspires to be, and the path he's chosen, but also who he's always been. Love, to self and to others.

Nurturers need to receive too.

This is maybe the single most common struggle that shows up among Nurturers. They're often so hardwired to give, when put in a situation where they must receive, the experience can feel brutally hard.

Remember Sarah Geddess, who runs Press + Post? She was going about her life, giving to her family, friends, clients, employees, causes, and local service initiatives. It was a lot, but she loved it. When giving is what makes you come alive, provided you're also giving to yourself, that tends to be your happy place. Then, in 2019, she was diagnosed with cancer in her jaw. She needed aggressive treatment, including complex surgery to reconstruct a significant part of her face. She didn't know if she'd ever eat or talk again, or live through it. In the blink of an eye, she went from someone who takes care of the world to someone who needed to ask for and receive care. That wasn't easy, even knowing how important it would be to her recovery.

Sarah, like so many Nurturers, has always had a lot of challenges receiving care from others. It almost feels like the very act goes against her reason for being. She's supposed to be the giver, not the taker. This orientation is common to Nurturers. But now she had to accept care, not just from her medical team, but family, friends, colleagues, even clients, in order to get through it. At a certain point, she realized, it was her time to be nurtured. If she didn't allow others in, there might not be a her there to take care of all the people she cared about down the road. She surrendered, but not entirely. Even during her treatment and recovery, she did something that for any non-Nurturer would seem completely contrary to healing and feeling better.

She felt a fierce need to do whatever she could to make sure those around her felt cared for. Her kids and husband, her employees and clients. For most others, this would be way too much outflow at a time when you need to fill your tank. But there's an odd glitch in this logic. Because Nurturers fill their tank and even come alive through giving, counterintuitively, doing what she could to take care of others at a time where she needed to surrender and receive a tremendous amount of care actually helped give her not just a focus, but a sense of purpose. It wasn't that she wanted to be distracted from her own suffering, it was that, in a way that only Nurturers can understand, the act of giving care is a powerful form of self-care.

That said, there are limits to this quirk's effectiveness, times where you become stretched so thin, the bump you get from filling others' tanks doesn't make up for the energy it takes. For Sarah, she finally hit that point where she just had to step into full-blown receiving mode and accept that, for a moment in time, she was the one most in need of love and support. For Nurturers to do the thing they're here to do, they also need to do the things that keep them whole, and allow others to help when they struggle to do it themselves.

SHOW ME THE MONEY.

Demand for the work of Nurturers—giving care—is high in nearly every domain in work and life. Suffering, whether experienced as mild unease or extreme pain, will always be an enduring fact of life. Because of that, there will always be a place for Nurturers.

In roles and careers more traditionally associated with giving care, like the practice of medicine, massage, and the healing arts, therapy, coaching, elder-care, health aides, and companionship, there is a clear path to income, either within an organization or industry or independently. Some are extremely well compensated.

Yet, like every other Sparketype, the Nurturer's full expression is not limited to any of these more traditional domains. What about the orderly or janitor in the hospital where the doctors and nurses work? Turns out, those who see themselves as part of the patient care experience not only make a bigger difference, but find a powerful sense of purpose beyond helping and cleaning. Nurturers may find a powerful outlet in teaching, either in schools, organizations, or even online. What about Nurturer baristas who love their customers? Or salespeople who create a safe space for clients to own their value and make nurturing decisions?

We saw how Teri Pruitt found an outlet as a dresser on Broadway and Billy as a videographer. That's the beauty of every Sparketype. You can find conventional ways to express your impulse and be compensated, but you can also almost always find an outlet in nearly any role, organization, or industry once you understand the impulse that is driving you.

While the work of Nurturers is in perpetual demand, how it is valued and how willing to be well compensated any given Nurturer is, well, that can be a bit more complicated. In the more conventional Nurturing professions, it is often highly valued and compensated. An experienced nurse or acupuncturist who is driven to give care may do very well. When this impulse finds an outlet in the corporate world, it often leads to not only a deeply loyal connection with colleagues and teams, but also high performance, which also may benefit the Nurturer by accelerating advancement and growth. When this impulse finds a path in less professional or even entirely nonprofessional domains, however, especially where it is not a stated part of the job, it may well be appreciated, but not rewarded or well compensated.

Nurturers may also feel conflicted about getting paid to do the thing they're here to do. This phenomenon is common with a number of other service-focused Sparketypes. For Nurturers, though, it can sometimes rise to the level of a near pathological self-flagellation. They may find themselves riddled with shame or guilt. How can they expect to earn money "on the back of other people's suffering"? Truth is, you did nothing to cause the suffering you're capable of easing, and willing to help release. There is value to the work your impulse fuels you to do. Just because others value that, and are willing to compensate you for that value, doesn't mean there's anything untoward about your willingness to step in and provide help at a moment someone needs it most. If you are never open to receiving appropriate value for the work you do, you will not be able to sustain yourself in the world and will find yourself doing something else. That will leave you feeling perpetually stifled and unfulfilled, and those you're capable of helping left to fend for themselves. Everyone loses. That said, there may well be circumstances where monetary compensation does not feel right, and may not be right.

Many Nurturers find powerful outlets for their work in non-professional, personal domains. Parenting, volunteering, reading to seniors, taking care of family and friends, these may all be deeply rewarding, valid, and valuable expressions of the Nurturer impulse that many Nurturers would never consider taking money for. They may not be compensated in a traditional monetary sense, but they do provide a powerful channel of expression for the Nurturer's impulse, and a strong sense of fulfillment and appreciation, often beyond what money ever could offer.

No matter what job, title, organization, or industry you're in or exploring, ask yourself, "Where is the opportunity for me to take care of others, lift them up, and let them feel seen, heard, held, and appreciated?" You may find or create these opportunities in ways you never saw, that may even lie outside the narrow confines of your job description, yet, without fail, they're almost always there. Then, expand beyond your main source of income, explore nurturing on the side, either for added income and fulfillment, or simply because it will add more of what makes you come alive to your life.

NURTURER

SPARK
YOUR WORK

Putting Your Sparketype to work.

You completed the Sparketype Assessment and discovered your Sparketype profile—your Primary, Shadow, and Anti-Sparketype. You understand what kind of work, on a DNA level, makes you come more fully alive, what empties you out and takes the most effort to do, and how it looks and feels when you do work that sparks you in a healthy, fully expressed way.

Now what?

What does this actually look like in the real world? How do I Spark my current work to make it feel a lot better? How do I find something different that is more likely to make me come alive? How do I find some blend of work that Sparks me?

Over at Spark Endeavors, we're continually deepening into these questions. Many of the answers have been shared in the individual Sparketype chapters, in the context of how each shows up and catches fire. This chapter gets more specific. It's about what your Sparketype looks like in the real world, in your work and life. We'll explore what I call the three Activation Keys. One is about getting expressive, one is about getting imaginative, and one is about getting expansive. Together, they're the Activation Trifecta.

EXPRESS.

Your Sparketype is like your Sparked-work DNA. It tells you, on a root level, what kind of work makes you come alive (or empties you out). For many, simply knowing this triggers all sorts of awakenings. You start to recognize moments, experiences, interactions, jobs, roles where your Sparketype has found an outlet. You also begin to see where you've been required to do things that are expressions of work that empties you out. Now, it's time to build on that early awakening and get granular.

You're going to create a living inventory of the specific ways you've expressed your Sparketype in the past. This will give you strong hints at what you might want to look for, do more of, and shy away from in the future.

YOUR SPARKETYPE EXPRESSION INVENTORY.

Your starting point is what I call the Sparketype Expression Inventory, or your SEI. You're going to look back at specific types of activities from your past that will help you identify certain tasks, tools, processes, practices, and topics that have served as powerful conduits to do the work of your Sparketype. Even when you had no idea that's what was really happening. Think about four different categories of work:

- Paid work (employee, contractor, professional, entrepreneur, etc.)
- Leisure/fun/craft, and other expressive activities
- Roles you've played (parent, volunteer, caretaker, etc.)
- Classes, courses of study

You may look at those categories and say, "Wait, only one of those is work!" Truth is, all of them require effort, sometimes in a fierce, hard, sustained way. And all hold the potential to let you invest yourself in experiences that make you come alive. So, you want to look at them all, because they may each play a role in your overall mix of work that Sparks you. Now, take out a piece of paper, journal, or any other app you use to take notes. Think about the first category—PAID WORK—then ask yourself:

What three experiences/roles/jobs, under this first category, made me feel most alive, most myself, like I was at my best most often, where I felt a genuine sense of purpose, like it mattered and I mattered, where I lost time because I was so engaged, when I felt most energized and excited, fully expressed, like I was accessing my true potential?

Write those three experiences down. If you have many more, write the three most compelling, the ones you feel emotionally when you think of them. And, if you have fewer than three, or none, that's okay, too. Remember, you're starting where you're starting, no judgments at all. You may find more of your hints about how to express your Sparketype from the other categories. For now, see if you can find ones that gave you at least some of the feelings described, or many of them at different times.

Okay, now for each of those three experiences (still under that first category), answer the following questions:

- What were the tasks you were doing when you felt most alive?
- What were the tools/tech/platforms you were using when you felt most alive?
- What were the processes you were engaged in when you felt most alive?
- What were the projects you were involved in when you felt most alive?
- What were the topics, subjects, or areas of focus, if relevant, you were focusing on when you felt most alive?

Feel free to modify the language of the prompts as needed. Write it all down, as much as you can remember. I know, it's going to take some work and some time. But here's the thing: this is the very work that becomes your fast-track to not just coming alive, but to freedom. It teases out the specific things you did that Sparked you and, equally valuable, it decouples them from any specific job, company, or industry. It focuses on the granular, often transferrable, experiences.

Why does that matter? Because it gives you the freedom to no longer be bound to old-school, traditional categories of work that may box you in, rather than free you up in your search for experiences, roles, organizations, or industries that make you come alive. Now, you can focus more on the specific activities that any opportunity might offer and not worry about whether it is "typically" known as the type of industry, organization, or role that people "like you" thrive in. As you'll see shortly, this wisdom will also equip you to potentially transform the work you're already doing and breathe new life into it.

When you're done with the first category, move on to each of the remaining three. Do the same thing for every category. Take the time to tease out exactly what it was about the experiences that Sparked you, that let you fully express your Sparketype and come alive. Once you've completed this process, maybe for the first time ever, you'll begin to understand what was really going on and why those moments and experiences felt so good (or bad). You'll have a living inventory—your Sparketype Expression Inventory—that will serve as a tool to deliver massively powerful hints and starting points for how to re-create those feelings when you look at the work you choose to do or not do from this point forward. This is where the Sparketype rubber hits the work road.

But, remember, this is critically important—your SEI is a living document that will expand over time. Your answers to the above questions are just your starting point. It's a list of powerful, personal hints about what has let you express your Sparketype in the past and will likely help you come alive in the future.

Your SEI is absolutely not an all-inclusive, complete document, especially when you first create it. It will continue to grow for life as you do more, experience more, try more things, and continue to add items to all the different categories. So hold it lightly, commit to continuing to grow it, and know that it is more about clarity and freedom than limitation.

Think of your SEI as an amazing starting point to discover, find, and do so much more of what makes you come alive, but do not limit yourself to looking only for work that offers the types of things on your SEI. Keep trying new things, running experiments to see what other tasks, tools, processes, practices, and topics you might be able to add that'll make you come alive over time. If you're considering a new opportunity and many of the things it'll require you to do are not on your list, and you've never really done them before, that doesn't mean they won't Spark you. It just means you don't yet know if they will or will not. It may be worth it to say *yes*, even if the only outcome is that you get to either expand your inventory, or know certain things aren't "your" things.

REIMAGINE.

———

Take a breath.

We humans are a quirky bunch. We sometimes do things, with the best of intentions, that set us up for failure, when all we want is success. Over the years, I've seen a self-destructive pattern emerge in so many people (yes, including in myself) in the context of work, especially work that empties us out. The intention isn't to cause self-harm or sabotage our careers. In fact, it's the exact opposite. Still, good intentions, bundled with painful work experiences, can sometimes lead to outcomes that are the exact opposite of what was hoped for. Nobody is immune. It's not about how smart or savvy or experienced you are, it's about a little glitch in human nature that sends you screaming to the exit door, before you realize you just might be complicit in causing your own unease.

———

Do not blow everything up.

Turns out, once you discover your Sparketype, then understand how to express it in work and life, it's not unusual to realize you're not doing many of the things that make you come alive. You think, "Now that I know what kind of work makes me come alive, why am I not doing it?!" Valid question! But here's where things often go off the rails. Instead of zooming the lens out and taking a bit of time to reflect, get honest, and put together an intentional and intelligent plan of action, you start to think, "It's so obvious that I'm doing the wrong thing; this is horrible. I need to make a big, disruptive change, and fast! I need to blow everything up and start over somewhere else!"

DO. NOT. DO. THAT!!!

Do *not* make big, likely painful, changes out of the gate. Do not blow up your career, business, or life in the name of getting all the "emptying" stuff out of your life and chasing all the "good, Sparky stuff." Do *not* take the vocational nuclear option. At least, not yet. And maybe (likely, even) never.

Yes, I get it. Once your eyes begin to open even a little to what makes you come alive, and you realize you're not doing it, there is an irresistible impulse to run from your current reality. Even if it's what is keeping a roof over your head. Even if the market is tight. Even if people around you think you've lost your mind.

And you're not alone. We tend to share this impulse en masse. There can be a strong tendency to convince yourself that the pain and disruption and financial upheaval of walking away is nothing in comparison to the existential angst of unfulfilled potential you currently feel. Maybe, earlier in life, there's truth to that. The stakes tend to be lower, you have less responsibility, more runway ahead of you to make things right if you mess up. The downside isn't quite as daunting.

The further into grown-up-hood you get, the more delusional that belief becomes. Sure, the suffering that comes from awakening to the work you're here to do, then realizing you're not doing it is real. It hurts. But you know what else is real? The very painful cost of dynamiting your current reality, the emotional groundlessness it can lead to, the fissures it often creates in your relationships, the relentless stress it can foster, and the devastating effect it can have on your emotional and physical health as you realize your next thing isn't dropping into your lap with quite the speed or ease you'd hoped. All too often, you underestimate the pain that comes from big, disruptive moves, and overestimate both the ease with which we'll "slide into" your next big thing and the way it'll make you feel (at least out of the gate).

Your rational brain knows this, and yet, so many of us consistently choose this delusion. There's a reason. Buying into it gives you the permission you so desperately seek to pursue the feeling you believe "your true destiny" will bring you, before you actually know how much, if any, of that projection is rooted in reality. Before you've done the work to understand the likely toll of a large-scale, disruptive, and immediate change.

We are often complicit, yet blind to it.

It gets worse. In a quest to conjure up the justification to cut and run that your rational brain wants to be able to point to (and tell your parents, friends, partners, and others when they ask if you've lost your marbles), you end up doing all sorts of things to subconsciously sabotage your current, non-Sparked jobs, careers, practices, or businesses. You do this unwittingly—yes, you don't even realize you're doing it—because it makes you feel better about walking away. It's easier to blow up a job or career you perceive as awful and stifling than it is to walk away from something that's not entirely working, yet may still have potential if you had the tools to fix it. That latter part takes work, and most of us don't yet have the tools. So, you start doing things, and framing things, without even realizing what you're doing, that make your current gig appear to be way less saveable or

Sparkable than it actually is. You tell yourself, "I hate it, and besides, it's not giving me what I need anyway," and continue to torpedo it at every turn, becoming complicit in making it bad enough to justify the pain of leaving.

Think about this: If you knew, with 100 percent certainty, the work you were doing today would have to be the very thing you did for the rest of your productive life, *but* you had the ability to reimagine the way you engaged with and experienced it, what would you do differently? How would you create the most purposeful and rewarding reality within those constraints? What would you do more of, and less of? Maybe you'd change the type of clients you work with, the service or product you offer, the way you get paid, the industry you serve, the tools or channels you use, the materials you work with, the mode of delivery or the people you work alongside. Maybe you'd cultivate a deeper understanding of compassion, social dynamics, and the human condition and learn to craft conversations and influence outcomes in a way that gives you more control and fulfillment. Maybe you'd invest in different alliances, skills, or try working on different projects or teams. Maybe you'd spend more time reorienting any number of other factors that, together, could make a profound change in the way you experience what is really the same thing, done differently.

Most of us never even think about this. We never try to right the ship by identifying what's not working, getting creative to change as much as we can, optimizing what is working, then building around that to make it as nourishing as possible *before* deciding "this'll never work, it's killing me" and then walking away. Instead, we do the exact opposite. We exacerbate the present-tense negatives in the name of justifying our escape. Then we hit *eject*. Prematurely. Occasionally it works. Especially earlier on, when, as we agreed, there's a lot less on the line. But more often than not, minutes, days, hours, or weeks after you've hit the *eject* button, the reality of this delusion sets in.

You find yourself not only mired in the profoundly underestimated pain of an existential implosion, but also deposited squarely into your new "supposedly" better reality, yet somehow, you are the same frustrated, stifled, unexpressed bundle of humanity, but with different paint on the walls and drapes on the windows. Bound to repeat the same patterns and inevitably shatter whatever temporary illusion of better you've run to.

You re-create the same morass of pain you've fled. In new clothes. On a new coast. In a new house. At a new job. With a new crew. And you continue to blame a world that feels perpetually positioned against you. Never realizing a simple fact. In the end, you are still the same un-flee-able you.

A different approach.

Consider a different first step. Instead of blowing up what lies outside, break open what lies within you. Before burning down your so-called malignant work experiences, first hit pause and take the time to look inside. To wake up. To embrace the thrash. To own your contribution to a status quo you so feverishly yearn to leave behind. Along with the grace, the blessings, the gifts, and resources you might reallocate to the task of "righting your own ship."

Then, ask what might happen if you stayed where you were, but did the work needed to reimagine and realign your current job, position, or role to allow you to more fully express your Sparketype, and do more of what fills you and less of what empties you.

Is this always possible? Not always, but far more often than our angsty impulse to cut bait might lead you to believe. There will be times where the best legitimate career or work option is, in fact, the nuclear option. There will be truly destructive, physically or psychologically harmful people and circumstances that must be abandoned. The abusive or horrifically toxic partner or culture. The physically and emotionally treacherous person, position, or place that is causing very real harm and is, for all intents and purposes, unfixable. At least by the mechanism of our own heart, hands, will, and being. In those cases, the pain of staying may be truly greater than the pain of leaving. Even if there is some level of your own work to be explored, you must first extract to a place of safety. Nothing I've shared is meant to suggest or in any way condone martyrdom, or encourage anyone to stay in the path of genuine harm. If you're not in a position to objectively discern whether this is happening, or have the insight or clarity needed to understand the difference, you need to ask for help from those who do.

At the same time, it's important to realize that these scenarios tend to be the rarer ones. More often than not, you discover the story you've been telling yourself about hating your current job, your partner, your people, your culture is just that. A story. One story. Not "the" story. A script rooted in a bit of truth that makes it easier to justify walking away and enduring the pain of disruption in the name of a future reality that you believe will "free" you, but may in fact be equally, if not more, fraught than the abyss out of which you seek so desperately to climb. You continue to look for the shiny and new, never realizing the feeling you so desperately lust after is less about what happens to you, and more about what comes from you.

Reimagine, resolve, realign.

Let's simplify the conversation to a job you feel is keeping you from your true destiny.

When you reframe your current career, practice, or venture in the light of the "constraint challenge" I offered above—make it as good as it can possibly get, before deciding whether to leave and start something new—it's not unusual for something unexpected to happen. Especially once you let go of the "this is awful, I have to bail" story.

- You start to do the work to make things better in a hundred tiny ways, and things begin to change.
- You recommit to taking meticulous care of your body, mind, heart, and soul. Some energy returns to you, and to the endeavor. You infuse the work with a new set of goals and aspirations.
- You begin to see ways to make it better that were often right in front of you before, but you conveniently looked past, because they didn't serve your desire to justify walking away.
- You examine the work of your Sparketype and hold it up to the work you are doing on a day-to-day basis in your current career, profession, or business.
- You search for ways to do less of the work that empties you and more of the work of your Sparketype, even if that means expanding beyond the bounds of a narrowly defined job description.
- You begin to integrate the specific tasks and processes, the actions and ideas that are the most organic expressions of your Sparketype.

- You find ways to spend more time working in the subject areas, domains, and topics that are extensions of your Sparketype.
- Most important, you begin the process of reclaiming control, taking action, and being intentional, expressed, and proactive, rather than stifled, reactive, and repressed.

Coming from a place of increasing alignment and agency now, you start to hold yourself differently, operate differently, work differently, take on different things that increasingly Spark you. The quality of your work and energy and ideas elevates. People notice and change how they relate to you in a thousand different ways.

Then, not infrequently, what you never thought possible happens. That thing you hated so fiercely starts to feel better. Instead of fleeing, you've learned to transform both the work and yourself. You've become an optimizer and alchemist, rather than a silent saboteur. This cultivates a deeper radiance, a sense of purpose. That inner light finds any number of pathways to expression and flow and connection and joy. You become Sparked. People around you begin to respond to the energy and presence you're putting out and you attract more opportunity to do more of the work that Sparks you, or continue to redefine the way you work to come more fully alive. It takes work, often hard work, to make this happen, but it also allows you to avoid the pain and disruption that would have come your way had you decided to take the "premature nuclear career option."

Truth is, you may still leave in the end. You may still find it's just not giving you what you need—but you make those choices on very different terms. You make them with a very different state of mind and, very likely, from a place that is so energetically, emotionally, and physically abundant with possibility and confidence that the doors that swing open would never have existed or been seen had you chosen to leave in the state of profound negativity that used to define your waking moments.

So, where does this leave you? Before you make that call to blow up your work and, along with it, potentially big pieces of your life, take stock. If you are in an extreme situation, do what you need to be okay. Get help, if you need it. But if what you're experiencing is a more existential crisis, bundled with a repeated pattern of people, jobs, companies, and the world letting you down or even battling against you, think more about reimagining and redefining what you do and how you do it than just blowing it all up. Think about the work of your Sparketype and how it might be expressed in your current work. Make it as good as it can get first. Then, even if you still choose to leave, you'll do it from a place of not only far greater conviction, but also embodied self-knowledge and the sense of alignment and radiance that often generates a level of possibility not available when your exit is more "cut and run" than "I did the work."

Sally.

Growing up, Sally Wolf (Advisor/Nurturer) was surrounded by summer camp. Her parents owned a store that outfitted campers every year. She went to camp the minute she was old enough, then became a counselor as soon as possible. It was the job she wanted, for life. Yet, somehow, she ended up getting an undergrad degree in psychology, two master's degrees in business and education, then building a twenty-year career as a high-powered media consultant.

Over the years, she began to realize that, for her, it was never about the strategy. She was good at it, really good, but it was always about the people. Working with amazing people, collaborating with them, mentoring and helping them grow, guiding clients, and building relationships that sustained often for years. She didn't love the work, but she loved being able to guide and take care of clients and colleagues, so she just kept on keeping on.

Everything was humming along, until she got cancer. Sally stepped back, took time to undergo treatment, and began a process of self-inquiry. She was trying to figure out what was next, but before she could, the cancer recurred. With her COBRA about to expire, she needed to figure something out. Leveraging her relationships, she landed a job at a media network, working on a small team with a senior vice president above her and a few other colleagues below her. She was back in the workforce, but driven largely by insurance coverage, not meaning or purpose. Many can relate.

Around the same time, Sally took the Sparketype Assessment and, discovering her Advisor Primary, a light bulb flipped on. Her job, ostensibly, was media strategy. Nothing in the job description spoke to guiding, mentoring, or taking care of people, but equipped with her Sparketype's validation of her lifelong impulse, she began spending time mentoring her younger teammates who were struggling with the team culture and a difficult dynamic with the person who led the team. She wasn't getting paid to coach or nurture her colleagues, but it felt natural to her; she loved doing it.

While the work in her job description was "fine," helping her colleagues made her come alive. One day, one of those teammates resigned. Sally played the role of team whisperer to her boss, sharing what had really happened. At the end of that conversation, even though he'd been very siloed about his personal life, she sensed something and asked him how he was. Disarmed, he opened up, shared some personal struggles that had been causing distress. With that, Sally did what she does. Tapping her Advisor/Nurturer impulse, she helped him through it. It wasn't part of her job; it was just the thing she couldn't not do. That moment changed him, and let her do more of what Sparked her.

Everyone noticed. People mentioned the change, and he gave Sally credit for planting the seeds and helping him along. Word spread, and other people started coming to her for coaching. She wanted to deepen her skills in this new domain, so she pursued coaching certification and took on a broader coaching role. She began loving work. Then, seeing an opening, Sally started talking to HR about creating coaching and positive psychology opportunities in-house. She began to build out group offerings and educational experiences, transitioning her focus into this area. When March 2020 hit and fear and anxiety ramped up, HR asked if she could do even more, so she started creating and leading programming, and coaching more individuals through that challenging moment. Armed with a deeper understanding of what made her come alive, Sally transformed a job started largely as a way to cover health insurance into a completely different one that she loved.

A few months later, with the media industry hit hard by the pandemic, Sally was let go. By then, it was more blessing than anything else. She launched her own consulting and training company and brought on her now former employer as her first consulting client. This all started when Sally said *yes* to a not-so-interesting job for a very mundane, security-driven reason, honed in on the tasks and activities that Sparked her, then looked for and acted upon the many opportunities to go beyond the scope of her job and do more of the work that made her come alive. In a fun way, now at the helm of her own business, she has effectively become a high-level camp counselor, but instead of kids and camps, her field of play is business executives and corporations.

Truth is, not all work is capable of reimagination, redefinition, and reclamation. So many people, however, find that when they hit pause and zoom the lens just far enough out of their current unhappiness to see with more clarity what's really going on, the opportunities to reimagine and redefine what they do are far more available than they thought. Before considering the nuclear career option (barring the case of a work experience that places you in the path of genuine physical or emotional harm), explore making your current gig as good as it can get. You just might be re-Sparked (or close enough), without having to endure the struggle, uncertainty, anxiety, and unease of a bigger, more disruptive change.

Even if you do end up leaving, you'll do it from a place of far more confidence, intentionality, and with a better understanding of why you're leaving and what you need to find or create for your next big adventure. This reframe, alone, is transformative for so many people.

EXPAND.

When we talk about work, what are we talking about?

Your SEI helps you begin to understand how your unique Sparketype shows up in specific ways in work and life, so you can make better choices about what to say *yes* or *no* to, and also no longer feel bound by conventional jobs, roles, organizations, or industries. Reimagining and realigning your current work with activities, experiences, and areas of interest that make you come alive lets you get more of what you need, without feeling the need to "blow anything up." Your final exploration focuses on how you define work. It's about the possibility of expanding your understanding of what actually counts as work, bigger picture, in the name of broadening your options for becoming Sparked through a vastly larger set of life experiences. This can be especially helpful when the thing you call your "job," even reimagined, redefined, and optimized, doesn't quite get you there.

We all live different lives with different responsibilities, constraints, limitations, fears, desires, hopes, aspirations, and values. Sometimes, there's a fairly direct, conventional path to work that Sparks you. Other times, you can reimagine and realign your work to give you more of what you need. Then, there are those times when conventional paths aren't easy to access and optimizing around your Sparketype gets you closer, but not entirely there. This sometimes happens when a deeply held value of financial security bumps up against a desire to come alive through your work, but there doesn't seem to be a high-probability, low-risk way to make it happen.

Rather than give up on the possibility of feeling fully Sparked, this is a great time to explore expanding your definition of work beyond simply what you get paid to do, and looking at a blend of paid full-time or part-time and non-paid experiences that, together, may well hold the potential to let you come alive.

Often, a certain blend of an "optimized" job or career, coupled with utterly Sparked side projects, jobs, hobbies, or other work can yield a deeply gratifying overall life. The "good-enough" day job gives you a sense of security and responsibility that allows you to honor the often sacredly held value of "financially supporting yourself and your family." It provides a regular paycheck, regular hours, mild cognitive and emotional cost, and plenty of time and energy to live well and devote your energies to other pursuits outside that work that do Spark you. And, you have the added benefit of not worrying whether they'll ever generate a dime.

From this place, you find yourself able to live each day in a way that, on balance, has substantial meaning, joy, and fulfillment, while also creating, solving, ordering, enlivening, or serving on a level that may well have been stifled had you made it not just the thing you can't not do, but the thing that also must put food on the table and a roof over your head.

***

It's a freedom thing.

Expanding your definition of the work that is available as the raw material to become Sparked gives you freedom. It lets you step into the greater truth, that we all come from different walks of life, with different circumstances and different abilities to contribute to the world in different ways. Some of those ways may become your primary source of income. Other channels of expression may generate revenue on the side. Still others may never yield any monetary compensation, but serve as very real paths to doing the thing you're here to do. When you look at the blend of opportunities to contribute and expand your definition of work to encompass all of these potential outlets for your Sparketype, you find yourself with a far greater abundance of options to come alive.

BE PATIENT WITH YOURSELF.

As you move through the process of Sparking your work and life, it's important to set expectations. The Sparketypes open your eyes. For some they're even revelatory and validating. But like every other assessment, tool, set of ideas, or programs, they are fairly blunt instruments. They reveal powerful, fundamental insights, then you need to do the work to refine what they're telling you to better reflect who you are as a unique being. Even then, expressing, refining, and integrating your Sparketype into your work and life is a deep-dive process that takes time. There are no quick fixes here. To promise some magical, instant result would be an insult to you, and to what you know deep down to be true. Making the journey from where you are now to building a living and life that is perpetually Sparked will take effort and time. It's important to know that up front, and embrace the journey as more of an adventure, a process of discovery.

Some insights may seem to drop into your mind almost immediately. When that happens, it's amazing! Other more nuanced and often valuable insights benefit from a bit of space, introspection, awareness, and sustained action over time. We all live different lives, have different circumstances, opportunities, limitations, responsibilities, and openness to possibility. Commit to the process, but also forgive your humanity. The best things in life take time and effort, but are worth the investment many times over. So, breathe into it. Keep doing the work. The reward is a lifetime of contribution that allows you to be more fully yourself, to come more fully alive, to experience greater freedom, not just at work, but in all parts of life.

SPARK YOUR LIFE,
SPARK THE WORLD

It's not just about coming alive,
it's about coming home.

Something tends to happen to us as we reach adulthood. We get lulled into the belief that living as your true self, working and offering and creating meaning and connection from that deepest part of yourself, is less important than toeing the line. We walk away from ourselves. Makers stop making. Performers stop bringing moments alive. Advocates quiet their impulse to champion. Nurturers stop giving care. Sometimes at the behest or command of others. Other times, because a sense of grown-up propriety or responsibility claims it. Often, it's more insidious.

We never actively decide to abandon who we are and the pursuits we knew as kids that Sparked us. It's more of a slow, unwitting surrender until, one day, years down the road, we find ourselves responsible, accomplished, yet empty. Wondering how life got away from us. When we stopped being that person we've always known ourselves to be.

We feel the weight of that abandonment. It shows up as an unshakable baseline of discontent, melancholy, disconnection, malaise, frustration. A pervasive sense that, somewhere along the line, we've lost ourselves. We don't entirely understand where it's coming from, but we feel it. And, in the moments where the stakes are high and life gets harder, uncertain, complicated—and it always will—we feel it even more. For many, we're taught and expected to ignore it. It becomes, simply, the ever-thickening air we breathe. It's just there. Laden with enough oxygen to let us function, yet perpetually wrapped in an invisible cloak of dysfunction. One we cannot remove, because it cannot be seen.

What I came to realize from the vast and rapidly growing archive of stories as thousands of new people discovered their Sparketypes every week is that, for many, this discontent had become their new normal. So many people had been living in a state of low-grade crisis their entire adult lives. A crisis of meaning. A crisis of joy. A crisis of excitement and enthusiasm. A crisis of purpose and expression. It'd just become an accepted part of life.

It's not that we don't work hard. We do. It's not that we don't "create output." We do. It's not that we don't "get things done." We do. We are mighty and beautiful and accomplished. It's that, for far too many, we work hard at something we could care less about. We create things that do not emanate from our souls. We get things done that matter to others, but little to us. And, even though we can turn back and point to the great work we've done, the litany of accomplishments, we still walk through life hollow. Just a touch sad. Unfulfilled. Living in a haze of pace, achievement, and exhaustion.

For millions who have stepped away from their essential nature, discovering their Sparketype can become an inciting incident. A call to discover, then embrace the work that makes them come alive, first as a salve for an anxious, isolated existence, then a reclamation. Turns out, honoring, then building around, your Sparketype is, in part, about making an unsatisfying working life a whole lot better. But it's about pulling the ripcord on a level of chronic, low-grade despair that has become so much a part of the fabric of our existence, we don't even realize we're wearing it.

Whether you do it as your living, on the side, or as an ingredient in some blend, your Sparketype is not just about coming alive, it's about coming home.

WE'VE MADE IT THIS FAR, THE BEGINNING OF MANY JOURNEYS . . .

The world of work, for most people, is anywhere from mildly to severely broken.

Nobody intended it to be this way. Honestly, nobody really benefits from it. We're all doing the best we can and, truth is, we are all in this together. There will be times where we feel more compelled and freer to focus on being Sparked, and other times where we're more in survival mode. There will be times where we need to just do what is necessary to take care of the bare necessities. Times where we have less control than we yearn for. Times where our aspirational needs for purpose, meaning, excitement, joy, expression, and flow will take a back seat to sustenance and security. Times where it won't be easy to become Sparked purely by the thing we get paid to do. Still, whether we're looking for work, employed but in a sustenance job, or well paid but flatlined, so many of us can get so much closer to the feeling of coming alive, being Sparked, than we thought possible.

If you're fully employed, explore how you might integrate your Sparketype into your current work. How might you reimagine or redefine the day-to-day elements, and possibly even the bigger scope of your work? How might you honor your commitments and acknowledge whatever circumstance you find yourself in and maybe even explore a more blended path to becoming Sparked? Reflect on the details of your Sparketype and think about the tasks, tools, and topics that give you that feeling of aliveness. Seek or create opportunities to bring more of those into what you do. Even in areas where these things do not fall squarely within the description of what you were hired to do, there are often ways to embrace them that are unseen to you until you start actively looking for them. If you're not currently working or under-employed, and you find yourself in a place of discovery for your next work adventure, this may be an understandably disconcerting, yet also sacred and powerful time to do this work. To learn more about what makes you come alive. To think about how you might create or find your next opportunity that brings as much "Sparked work" into what you do as possible. Or to create the space to make it happen on the side. Look for the indicators, the signs from past experiences or current yearnings that align with your Sparketype when you're considering what to explore, what to say *yes* or *no* to. They matter, often more than we realize. If some are there, but not all, consider how you might bring more of what you want (and whether you have the power to do that) into the experience.

No matter where you go from here, an invitation—don't turn away from the road you've begun to walk down when you said *yes* to discovering your Sparketype. *Yes* to sharing it with friends, family, colleagues, and collaborators, and asking them to discover theirs. *Yes* to diving into this book. *Yes* to taking steps, even baby steps, to come more fully alive in whatever way is accessible to you. *Yes* to fanning the flames and bringing more meaning, expression, flow, purpose, and possibility into your work and life.

Right now, you need that. And so does the world. We need people who've stepped back into a place of possibility and potential. We need people who are fully alive, maximally capable and fired up, tapping everything they have from a place of joy and enthusiasm to create the next generation of ideas, solutions, services, platforms, institutions, and experiences that will lead us all into the future in a more empowered, activated, and alive way. We need organizations and leaders, fueled by the unleashed potential, purpose, drive, expression, and energy of a fully Sparked workforce, to serve as centers for innovation, growth, and the furtherance not just of industry, but of culture, society, and the unbridled elevation of every individual who contributes to the quest. Not just because *we* want to feel better, but because the depth and complexity of the challenges we face *demand* the best we have to offer. When we show up Sparked, we come alive, and the world comes along with us.

This is bigger than us. It's time for a reclamation of work as a source of meaning, energy, purpose, joy, and potential. And every individual plays a part. Beyond the awakenings and invitations to activate your own Sparketype, do one simple thing. Invite one person, maybe two, three would be great . . . okay, just invite everyone you know . . . to become Sparked. It starts with a simple, fun step. Just ask them to discover their Sparketype. Along the way, we'll grow a community, a movement of human beings around the world on a mission to come alive and radiate that energy, that sense of purpose and possibility, to everyone around us. To do well and do good. To change the way we work and live. And, along the way, the state of the world as we know it.

Together we can spark the world! One lit-up human at a time.

APPENDIX

The Satisfaction Spectrum™.

On the surface, the first step to becoming Sparked—to coming more fully alive—is to do more things that allow you to express your Sparketype. On a deeper level, there's a more nuanced and powerful awakening that adds to your understanding. Once you learn it, it'll explain so much about past experiences, and also help you more easily discern what to say *yes* or *no* to in the future. It may also, surprisingly, open up a wellspring of self-forgiveness and allow you to release unjustly accumulated shame.

All ten Sparketypes exist along what's known as the Satisfaction Spectrum.

On one side of the spectrum are Sparketypes that are fully expressed and most readily satisfied by a more internally oriented focus on process, like creation, problem-solving, learning, and distilling. The results of their work often serve and impact others in meaningful, sometimes groundbreaking ways. That's a great thing, it's meaningful, something they enjoy knowing, and it is often that outcome side that is connected directly to professional advancement. At the same time, though they might never say it out loud in polite company, that's not the main reason they do it. It's the process, itself, that Sparks them.

The other side of the spectrum is increasingly externally oriented. It is about service to others, impact, and outcomes. The fact that they've developed expertise in some process or

Satisfaction Spectrum for the Ten Sparketypes

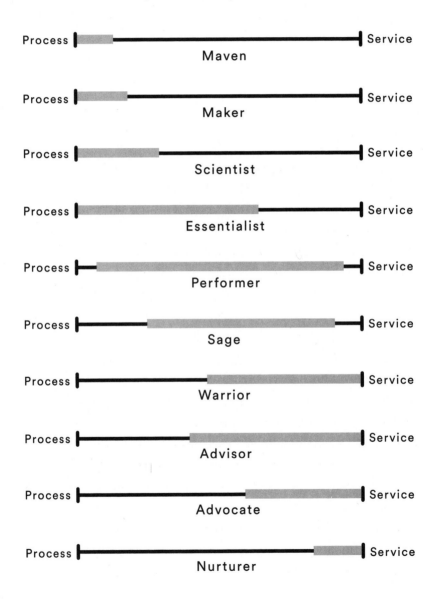

mastered a craft along the way is far less meaningful than the simple knowledge that they've been of service. That's what they live for. To elevate others.

Each Sparketype represents a certain range along the Satisfaction Spectrum, some more readily fulfilled by pure process, others by pure service, and still others spanning the middle.

WHY DOES THIS MATTER?

Are there outliers? Of course, there always are. Still, knowing whether you're more expressed and fulfilled by process or service or some blend helps you better understand how to come alive. If you happen to be fueled by a Sparketype that lies more strongly on the process side of the equation, it may also free you from a bit of multigenerational baggage.

There's an old line that holds the only path to a meaningful, purpose-filled, fully expressed living or life is service. For some, especially those with Sparketypes that lie on the service side of the Satisfaction Spectrum, that is largely true. Without service in the mix, you literally cannot do the thing you're here to do. For process-driven Sparketypes, however, the understanding that what you do is of service to others, that it affects or impacts them, is "nice," maybe even makes you feel pretty good, but it's not the core reason you do what you do. For you, its central role is to serve as feedback, validation of your level of excellence and expertise in the process that both fuels and nourishes you, and also happens to serve others. The simple opportunity to immerse yourself in the process, fully resourced and unimpeded, is what holds your greatest reward and opportunity for expression. It's not about being selfish or ego-driven; it's simply that you get nearly all you need to feel Sparked through a more inward-facing process, even when the output from it moves, serves, and elevates others. And that's okay.

This does not negate or deny the very real value and benefits of everyone, on some level, doing things that benefit others. The net positive effect on society is real and meaningful. We all want to live in a world that exalts caring for each other. As a general ethos, we all benefit from giving and receiving kindness. On a more psychological level, when you become other-focused, it helps break the cycle of neuroses and the anxiety that often consumes you when all you think about is yourself. It is hard to maintain the spin of self-defeating and often self-flagellating self-talk when you force your focus toward others. Plus, often, those you'd help elevate are, on some level, in more need than you. Finding yourself confronted with this reality in a very human, face-to-face way can bring you back to a state of gratitude. Givers don't just help others rise, they also benefit from elevated mood that often lasts days beyond the act of giving. Again, the net effect is you rise, and others rise. We should all help others, if for no other reason than it weaves the fabric of a kinder, more connected world, one we all want to inhabit. But it's important to distinguish these broader, societal motivators for service from the dated and, at least for those whose Sparketypes lie on the process side of the spectrum, shame-inducing overlay that says the only "valid" work and way to come alive is service.

Rather than shaming anyone for their ability to come alive through means other than direct service, maybe it's time to just acknowledge that we all derive meaning, purpose, and experience passion and joy from different things and in different ways, and that's okay.

YOUR ANTI-SPARKETYPE.

Each of the ten Sparketypes speaks to a specific type of work. When that work is your Primary or Shadow, it plays a meaningful role in making you come alive. As a general rule, the more you can do it, the better! Build your work and life around it and you become Sparked.

But here's the thing. Any one of those same Sparketypes can also play the role of your Anti-Sparketype. In that way, it becomes the work that empties you out. The work that you generally loathe the most, that feels like it's always a slog, even when you're somewhat accomplished at it, the work that takes the most motivation to do, and leaves you the most drained.

For example, when your Primary Sparketype is the Essentialist, creating order from chaos, distilling, simplifying, creating systems and processes may be hard work, but it also nourishes, energizes, and fills you up. It Sparks you. If that very same role is your Anti-Sparketype, then doing that work, even if it's objectively easier, feels so much harder, and leaves you so much more depleted.

You've probably sensed what kind of work falls under your Anti-Sparketype, the same way you've had an intuitive knowing about the type of work that makes you come alive. Even if not, the great news is, you don't have to guess. The first version of the Sparketype Assessment was developed to reveal your Primary and Shadow. A few years into our research, we realized we'd also done 90 percent of the work of being able to discern and share your Anti-Sparketype as well. We went back into the lab and developed a new, more robust algorithm that discerns and reports not just your Primary and Shadow Sparketypes, but also your Anti-Sparketype.

If you were one of the early assessment-takers, feel free to complete the currently available version, so that you have the added benefit of knowing not just your Primary and Shadow, but also your Anti-Sparketype. This added insight reveals why certain work lands with such unease, takes so much out of you, and helps show you the work you may want to hand off to others whose Sparketypes are more aligned, if and when possible. It's also a very powerful data-point for leaders who are working to understand how to best align people with work that makes them come alive, and avoid work that empties them out.

- **When the Maven is your Anti-Sparketype,** the process of acquiring knowledge, of deep learning or the pursuit of a fascination for no reason beyond the joy of the pursuit of knowledge, leaves you largely uninterested, disengaged, and emptied out. You'll embrace learning, if you have to, but it's almost always about having to learn something because it allows you to do something else, rather than the pure love of acquiring knowledge for knowledge's sake.
- **When the Maker is your Anti-Sparketype,** the process of taking ideas and turning them into something real, be it digital, physical, or experiential, leaves you flatlined. When faced with the need to immerse yourself in a process of creation or making, even if you understand its value, it just feels like such a heavy and maybe even scary lift. All you want to do is find a way for someone else to take the lead, or rush through it as fast as you can so you can be done with it.
- **When the Scientist is your Anti-Sparketype,** the invitation to spend all your time and energy grappling with burning questions, figuring out complex problems, or solving puzzles leaves your head spinning and your spirit plummeting. You'll do it, and maybe

even develop the skills needed to excel, but it is never the thing that comes most naturally and it's the pursuit that takes the most out of you and leaves you emptiest.

- **When the Essentialist is your Anti-Sparketype,** the very thought of having to spend time and energy creating order, systems, processes, checklists, simplicity, or any type of order from chaos makes you want to run in the other direction. That doesn't mean you don't love when those systems and simplicity and clarity exist, you often do, and benefit greatly from them. You just want nothing to do with creating, then maintaining them.

- **When the Performer is your Anti-Sparketype,** the idea of being front and center, having to take the stage, be it a business meeting, pitch, theatrical performance, speech, sales call, or any other engagement, interaction, or moment that calls for a certain level of animation, energy, enlivenment, or entertainment, is an incredibly unpleasant thought. You may well train to become skilled at it, but even though you enjoy seeing progress and get more comfortable, it is still likely to be the thing you least want to do and the experience that takes the most out of you and requires the greatest space for recovery.

- **When the Sage is your Anti-Sparketype,** the work of illumination, figuring out how to share what you know and turn on the lights of insight, knowledge, discovery, and awakening takes a lot out of you. You understand the benefits and often love being on the other side of that equation, and you may even develop some proficiency in the process of illumination that helps it not feel like such a heavy lift and adds in the feeling of competence. Yet, at the end of the day, the work will likely never come close to giving you the feeling and energy and release potential that comes with doing the work of your Primary and Shadow.

- **When the Warrior is your Anti-Sparketype,** the work of bringing people together, whether only a few in a local setting, friends, family, or larger groups, teams, cohorts, communities, divisions, organizations, then leading them on some adventure, quest, journey, or endeavor, takes the life right out of you. You may love being invited along and participating, once someone else has gathered people together, set the course, and is leading them, but the idea of you being that person is not fun. You may become highly skilled at this work, and you may care deeply about the people and the outcome and be called upon to take on this role, but the work, itself, and the process of gathering and leading, always feels hard and takes more out of you than it gives you.

- **When the Advisor is your Anti-Sparketype,** the work of guiding, mentoring, coaching, or working in an intimate, hands-on way to guide people or groups through a process of growth and toward an outcome is something that feels perpetually onerous to you. Like all other Sparketypes, you may well acquire the skill of being good at it over time, and that may make it feel like it comes easier, but it will likely always feel like a much heavier lift, and leave you emptier than the work of your Primary and Shadow.

- **When the Advocate is your Anti-Sparketype,** taking on the role of championing, advocating for, and shining the light on an underrepresented idea, ideal, individual, or community leaves you not just flatlined, but often completely emptied out. It's not just that the work of advocacy is hard, it's that it also tends to war with your wiring and, even if you do the work to learn the craft and become accomplished, it will likely always take so much out of you and never approach the enlivening experience of doing the work of your Primary and Shadow, even when those may be very hard, too.

- **When the Nurturer is your Anti-Sparketype,** you may become competent or even very good at the work of giving care, nurturing, and uplifting others. They may feel the impact of your efforts and you enjoy that and may care a lot about those you touch. But, for you, while you appreciate the benefits and the effect on others, the work often feels like it takes everything out of you and leaves you feeling like you're perpetually in need of recovery.

In reading this book, look up your Primary and Shadow Sparketype, and read those chapters. Then, look up your Anti-Sparketype and remember, when it's in the role of Anti-Sparketype, this is not the work that fills you, but rather empties you. The struggles associated with each will likely be that much more amplified when you seek to do this work. Becoming skilled at it can help, because the feeling of competence can help offset the experience of depletion. But it rarely approaches the feeling the work of your Primary and Shadow gives you, and often leaves you in the exact opposite state.

Still, there will be times all of us will have to do this work, on some level. As an entrepreneur for my entire adult life, I've had to do the work of all ten Sparketypes at various times, because starting a company demanded it and I didn't have the resources to have anyone else do it. If you find yourself in a circumstance where you cannot quickly or easily remove the work of your Anti-Sparketype from your job, all is not lost. Work on ways to minimize the work of your Anti-Sparketype, delegate, or if possible outsource as much as you can. Find others whose Primary or Shadow is your Anti-Sparketype and see if there is a way you might be able to "trade up" so you're both more lit up. Explore other ways to do more of the work that makes you come alive, even on the side or as hobbies or fun activities, outside the confines of the work you get paid to do. This has the effect of both filling you up with activities that Spark you, and also helping counter the draining effect of your Anti-Sparketype.

At the end of the day, the more informed you are, the more able you are to make choices that Spark you.

PREVALENCE.

Ever wonder how many others share your Primary or Shadow Sparketype, or your pairing? Turns out, you're not alone. It's one of the most frequently asked questions. How much of the population is like me? How rare or unusual am I? While we cannot tell you how you compare to the entirety of the human race, we can share some pretty compelling data from the fast-growing universe of Sparketype Assessment–takers from around the world. As of this writing, that represents a sample of about five hundred thousand people. Here's what we've learned.

APPENDIX

PRIMARY SPARKETYPE	PREVALENCE
Advisor	10%
Advocate	8%
Essentialist	7%
Maker	17%
Maven	26%
Nurturer	13%
Performer	3%
Sage	6%
Scientist	7%
Warrior	2%

SHADOW SPARKETYPE	PREVALENCE
Advisor	11%
Advocate	6%
Essentialist	9%
Maker	12%
Maven	26%
Nurturer	11%
Performer	4%
Sage	9%
Scientist	10%
Warrior	2%

PRIMARY/SHADOW PAIRINGS	PREVALENCE
Advisor/Advocate	0.6%
Advisor/Essentialist	0.6%
Advisor/Maker	0.5%
Advisor/Maven	2.3%
Advisor/Nurturer	2.6%
Advisor/Performer	0.3%
Advisor/Sage	2.2%
Advisor/Scientist	0.4%
Advisor/Warrior	0.4%
Advocate/Advisor	1.0%
Advocate/Essentialist	0.5%
Advocate/Maker	0.6%
Advocate/Maven	2.2%
Advocate/Nurturer	2.2%
Advocate/Performer	0.3%
Advocate/Sage	0.5%
Advocate/Scientist	0.6%
Advocate/Warrior	0.3%
Essentialist/Advisor	0.5%
Essentialist/Advocate	0.3%
Essentialist/Maker	1.0%

PRIMARY/SHADOW PAIRINGS	PREVALENCE
Essentialist/Maven	2.3%
Essentialist/Nurturer	0.7%
Essentialist/Performer	0.1%
Essentialist/Sage	0.5%
Essentialist/Scientist	1.2%
Essentialist/Warrior	0.2%
Maker/Advisor	0.8%
Maker/Advocate	0.6%
Maker/Essentialist	1.8%
Maker/Maven	8.2%
Maker/Nurturer	1.5%
Maker/Performer	1.3%
Maker/Sage	0.7%
Maker/Scientist	1.9%
Maker/Warrior	0.3%
Maven/Advisor	2.3%
Maven/Advocate	1.5%
Maven/Essentialist	3.2%
Maven/Maker	5.9%
Maven/Nurturer	2.8%
Maven/Performer	0.9%

PRIMARY/SHADOW PAIRINGS	PREVALENCE
Maven/Sage	3.5%
Maven/Scientist	5.3%
Maven/Warrior	0.3%
Nurturer/Advisor	3.3%
Nurturer/Advocate	2.2%
Nurturer/Essentialist	1.1%
Nurturer/Maker	1.3%
Nurturer/Maven	3.6%
Nurturer/Performer	0.4%
Nurturer/Sage	0.9%
Nurturer/Scientist	0.4%
Nurturer/Warrior	0.1%
Performer/Advisor	0.3%
Performer/Advocate	0.2%
Performer/Essentialist	0.2%
Performer/Maker	1.1%
Performer/Maven	1.0%
Performer/Nurturer	0.4%
Performer/Sage	0.2%
Performer/Scientist	0.1%
Performer/Warrior	0.1%

PRIMARY/SHADOW PAIRINGS	PREVALENCE
Sage/Advisor	1.7%
Sage/Advocate	0.2%
Sage/Essentialist	0.5%
Sage/Maker	0.4%
Sage/Maven	2.1%
Sage/Nurturer	0.5%
Sage/Performer	0.2%
Sage/Scientist	0.3%
Sage/Warrior	0.2%
Scientist/Advisor	0.3%
Scientist/Advocate	0.3%
Scientist/Essentialist	1.3%
Scientist/Maker	0.9%
Scientist/Maven	3.7%
Scientist/Nurturer	0.2%
Scientist/Performer	0.1%
Scientist/Sage	0.3%
Scientist/Warrior	0.2%
Warrior/Advisor	0.5%
Warrior/Advocate	0.2%
Warrior/Essentialist	0.2%

PRIMARY/SHADOW PAIRINGS	PREVALENCE
Warrior/Maker	0.1%
Warrior/Maven	0.3%
Warrior/Nurturer	0.1%
Warrior/Performer	0.1%
Warrior/Sage	0.3%
Warrior/Scientist	0.2%

Interestingly, knowing how common or rare your Primary, Shadow, and pairing is, is fascinating on an individual level. When we work with organizations, this wisdom takes on a whole new depth of importance. We are able to map prevalence ratios across teams, divisions, and entire organizations, which can be incredibly eye-opening. It helps explain certain outcomes and dynamics, and also, not infrequently, identifies potential areas of imbalance or gaps in innate impulse and skills. This can be highly useful in better understanding how to effectively lead, inspire, motivate, and elevate the experience of work and the quality of outcomes.

SPARKED RESOURCES

FAQS.

Got questions that weren't answered in the book? Visit Sparke-type.com/faq, where you can check out our growing list of Fre-quently Asked Questions, along with in-depth answers and, if you like, even propose your own questions. Here are a handful of the most common questions you'll find answers to there:

- Where does your Sparketype come from?
- What is the methodology/basis behind the Sparketypes?
- How is it related to flow, meaning, purpose, engagement, and performance, and is there data around it?
- Is your Sparketype the same thing as your passion?
- How is motivation different from your Sparketypes?
- What if your Primary and Shadow Sparketype don't seem like they'd work well together?
- Can you be super-accomplished without being Sparked?
- Is your Sparketype what you're good at, or skilled at?
- Can your Sparketype change over time, or is it fixed?
- What if you don't like/want your Sparketype? What if your Sparketype *does* ring true, but you don't *want* it to?

- Is your ability to do the work of your Sparketype limited by your job title, company, or industry?
- How do the Sparketypes compare to other major typing systems, like MBTI, Strengthsfinder, and so on?

FOR INDIVIDUALS.

With the global community of Sparked humans expanding at a rapid rate, we are in regular conversation with our community, inquiring how best to be of service and provide useful and valuable support and solutions. These range from virtual workshops, courses, and trainings to in-person experiences. You can check out our currently available resources, tools, and programs, and see if any might accommodate your needs at sparketype.com/ind.

FOR LEADERS AND ORGANIZATIONS.

This book is, in no small part, a primer for individuals to go deeper into their personal Sparketype profiles and better understand how to get more out of work and life. That said, the concepts, tools, and technologies have powerful application in organizations as well. We've worked with everyone from startup founders to emerging and senior leaders, executives, and C-level teams at global enterprises, with a focus on tapping the Sparketypes to empower leaders to be more effective, increase engagement and motivation, enhance purpose and performance, and facilitate better communication and understanding.

Engagements range from outcome-specific licensed programming, deployed via LMS to in-person or virtual workshops, off-sites, keynotes, team and organization profiles and insights, and more. To learn more about possible organizational offerings and engagements, visit sparketype.com/org.

FOR HELPING PROFESSIONALS.

As the Sparketypes began rapidly spreading around the world, we began to hear from helping professionals who saw the value of the Sparketypes both in their own lives and work, and also in their application as a powerful new tool to bring to their work with clients. Everyone from coaches, consultants, and facilitators to teachers, administrators, and L&D professionals reached out to inquire about varying levels of support, training, certification, and licensing. We love to see this work ripple out into the world, but are also committed to supporting a high standard of care as it does. So we've created a variety of opportunities to learn more and be supported and accredited for use in professional contexts. To learn more about available opportunities, visit sparketype.com/pros.

INDEX

INDEX

INDEX

INDEX

ABOUT THE AUTHOR

JONATHAN FIELDS is a dad, husband, award-winning author, executive producer, and host of one of the top-ranked podcasts in the world, *Good Life Project*®, which has been featured everywhere from the *Wall Street Journal* to *Oprah Magazine* and even Apple's iconic annual product event.

He is also the founder of a number of wellness companies. His current focus is on being founder and CEO of Spark Endeavors and lead architect behind the Sparketypes®. This is an archetyping system and set of tools tapped by an expansive, rapidly growing community of individuals and organizations to identify, embrace, and cultivate work that makes people come alive and equips organizations and leaders to more effectively unlock purpose, potential, and joy.

Jonathan speaks and facilitates globally for groups and organizations of all sizes. His work has been featured widely in the media, including the *New York Times*, *FastCompany*, the *Wall Street Journal, Inc.*, *Entrepreneur*, *Forbes*, *Oprah Magazine*, *Elle*, *Allure*, the *Guardian*, and more.

LEARN MORE AND CONNECT

SPARKETYPE.COM
(sparketype-related)

GOODLIFEPROJECT.COM
(podcast listen & learn)

JONATHANFIELDS.COM
(speaking & reading)